T0208652

The Gospel: Love Divine

William H. Wetmore

WESTBOW
PRESS
A DIVISION OF THOMAS NELSON
& ZONDERVAN

Scriptures taken from the Holy Bible, New International Version®, NIV®.
Copyright © 1973, 1978, 1984, 2011 by Biblica, Inc.™ Used by permission of
Zondervan. All rights reserved worldwide. www.zondervan.com The "NIV"
and "New International Version" are trademarks registered in the United
States Patent and Trademark Office by Biblica, Inc.™ All rights reserved.

Revised Standard Version of the Bible, copyright 1952 [2nd edition, 1971] by
the Division of Christian Education of the National Council of the Churches of
Christ in the United States of America. Used by permission. All rights reserved.

WestBow Press books may be ordered through booksellers or by contacting:

WestBow Press
A Division of Thomas Nelson & Zondervan
1663 Liberty Drive
Bloomington, IN 47403
www.westbowpress.com
1 (866) 928-1240

Because of the dynamic nature of the Internet, any web addresses or
links contained in this book may have changed since publication and
may no longer be valid. The views expressed in this work are solely those
of the author and do not necessarily reflect the views of the publisher,
and the publisher hereby disclaims any responsibility for them.

Any people depicted in stock imagery provided by Thinkstock are models,
and such images are being used for illustrative purposes only.
Certain stock imagery © Thinkstock.

ISBN: 978-1-4908-5059-7 (sc)
ISBN: 978-1-4908-5061-0 (hc)
ISBN: 978-1-4908-5060-3 (e)

Library of Congress Control Number: 2014915896

Printed in the United States of America.

WestBow Press rev. date: 10/30/2014

Consider Abraham: "He believed God, and it was credited to him as righteousness." Understand, then, that those who believe are children of Abraham. The Scripture foresaw that God would justify the Gentiles by faith, and announced the gospel in advance to Abraham: "All nations will be blessed through you." So those who have faith are blessed along with Abraham, the man of faith. (Gal 3:6-9)

The god of this age has blinded the minds of unbelievers, so that they cannot see the light of the gospel of the glory of Christ, who is the image of God. (2 Cor 4:4)

For God so loved the world that he gave his one and only Son, that whoever believes in him shall not perish but have eternal life. For God did not send his Son into the world to condemn the world, but to save the world through him. Whoever believes in him is not condemned, but whoever does not believe stands condemned already because he has not believed in the name of God's one and only Son. This is the verdict: Light has come into the world, but men loved darkness instead of light because their deeds were evil. Everyone who does evil hates the light, and will not come into the light for fear that his deeds will be exposed. But whoever lives by the truth comes into the light, so that it may be seen plainly that what he has done has been done through God." (John 3:16-21)

I [Paul] am not ashamed of the gospel, because it is the power of God for the salvation of everyone who believes: first for the Jew, then for the Gentile. For in the gospel a righteousness from God is revealed, a righteousness that is by faith from first to last, just as it is written: "The righteous will live by faith." (Rom 1:16-17)

Contents

The Gospel of Christ: Its Message (Romans 1:17)

Part 3. Epilogue

The Gospel: Love Divine

Preface

The gospel of God is the divine message of God's holy love for His Creation. The gospel is the good news of God's love, of faith, of redemption and reconciliation, of salvation, of resurrection, of judgment, and of eternal life for those who believe in Him.

Its purpose is to reestablish the holiness and righteousness of all that He had made. God defined everything He made as *good*. However, sin came into the world, leading to evil and wickedness on the earth.

The LORD saw how great man's wickedness on the earth had become, and that every inclination of the thoughts of his heart was only evil all the time. The LORD was grieved that he had made man on the earth, and his heart was filled with pain. So the LORD said, "I will wipe mankind, whom I have created, from the face of the earth — men and animals, and creatures that move along the ground, and birds of the air — for I am grieved that I have made them." (Gen 6:5-8)

God sent the Flood to accomplish what He had decreed.

However, God sought to reestablish His holiness and His righteousness in His Creation and to redeem and reconcile sinners to Himself. This is the gospel, the good news, of which God is the Origin.

As such, God has sent forth the gospel of His Son which began with the message announced to Abraham and concluded with the promise of a New Heaven, a New Earth, and a New Jerusalem.

There is only one gospel, the gospel of Christ.

As such, the gospel of Christ is the fundamental message of Scripture. All other biblical messages revolve around the gospel; all other biblical messages reinforce and support the gospel.

The gospel is the revelation of God's will for mankind for eternity.

The gospel is God's beacon of light in an otherwise dark and sinful world.

The gospel is good news of great joy.

There are many people throughout history who have denied God and His will for His Creation. They deny His sovereignty and His authority; they reject His love; they deny the Cross of Christ; they deny the power of the Holy Spirit. There are those who accept and those who reject the gospel. This is the eternal war for the hearts, souls, and minds of mankind.

So the gospel calls mankind to a time of decision: to accept or reject God.

There will be persecution because of the rejection of the gospel of Christ.

There is darkness and evil in the world. Into that darkness comes the light of the gospel. It has always been so; it will always be so until the Final Judgment and the End of the Age.

In the meantime, Christians are to proclaim the gospel, in spite of opposition.

However, God is sovereign, and His gospel message will prevail, regardless of the defiant acts of any human being. What the gospel declares is what the God of the Universe will achieve.

Everyone must hear the gospel. That is why the understanding of the gospel is so important; that is why the gospel must be preached regardless of the consequences. We are to be God's messengers; the Holy Spirit is to convince and convict.

The gospel prepares us for ministry; the gospel prepares us for this life; the gospel prepares us for eternity. The gospel prepares us to be the children of God, to become a new creation (Gal 6:15) and to grow into the image of God (Gen 1:27).

The gospel is the fulfillment of divine promises made and divine promises fulfilled.

In essence, the gospel is basically *good news of great joy from God.* It is good news for the righteous; it is bad news for unrepentant sinners.

God's gospel is an unfolding of truths, reflecting His will and plan for the redemption and reconciliation of His creation. He gives us more knowledge of His will as our relationship with Him grows.

God gives us such knowledge, not so that we would know more, but rather that we would do more.

Knowledge of the gospel and its message are essential to understanding the very nature of God and our life as His children. The gospel defines our past, present, and future. It defines salvation; it defines eternity.

As saints of God, the application of the gospel message to our lives and in God's world is essential for our lives as the children of God.

Our faith will grow as our understanding of the gospel increases. In addition, we will live lives more pleasing to God when we understand and apply the gospel of God in all that we do and say.

We are to proclaim the gospel. By such actions, we will advance the Kingdom of God. One leads to the other.

The purpose of this book is to explain the gospel of God in terms that will equip all Christians to know the truth of the gospel and to be prepared to explain the gospel to those who have not yet believed in Christ nor received Him as Savior and Lord.

This book is also written to challenge non-believers to address the meaning of their lives and to present an opportunity to come to God for the redemption and reconciliation that He alone can provide.

Above all, Christians are to present the light of the gospel to a dark and evil world.

The Christian church is on a rescue mission.

However, in the midst of the evil that has been present in every age, there is the faithful witness of the great champions of faith who have been steadfast and stood firm in proclaiming the gospel.

Then Jesus came to them and said, "All authority in heaven and on earth has been given to me. Therefore go and make disciples of all nations, baptizing them in the name of the Father and of the Son and of the Holy Spirit, and teaching them to obey everything I have commanded you. And surely I am with you always, to the very end of the age." (Matt 28:18-20)

But you will receive power when the Holy Spirit comes on you; and you will be my witnesses in Jerusalem, and in all Judea and Samaria, and to the ends of the earth. (Acts 1:8)

Grace and peace to you from God our Father and the Lord Jesus Christ, who gave himself for our sins to rescue us from the present evil age, according to the will of our God and Father, to whom be glory forever and ever. Amen. (Gal 1:3-5)

To God be the glory—great things He has done.

William H. Wetmore

Chapter 1

Introduction

The angel of the LORD called to Abraham from heaven a second time and said, "I swear by myself, declares the LORD, that because you have done this and have not withheld your son, your only son, I will surely bless you and make your descendants as numerous as the stars in the sky and as the sand on the seashore. Your descendants will take possession of the cities of their enemies, and through your offspring all nations on earth will be blessed, because you have obeyed me." (Gen 22:15-18)

The god of this age has blinded the minds of unbelievers, so that they cannot see the light of the gospel of the glory of Christ, who is the image of God. (2 Cor 4:4)

This grace was given us in Christ Jesus before the beginning of time, but it has now been revealed through the appearing of our Savior, Christ Jesus, who has destroyed death and has brought life and immortality to light through the gospel. (2 Tim 1:9-10)

The gospel of Christ is the greatest message in Scripture, containing the ultimate divine truths for Christians in particular and for the world in general.

The gospel offers union of redeemed man with the holy God.

The biblical passages at the beginning of this chapter present truths about the gospel of Christ that reflects its overall purpose and character.

Genesis 22:15-18 identifies the *universal* character of the gospel: *through your offspring all nations on earth will be blessed. Through your [Abraham] offspring* means that this blessing will come through Abraham: notice that *offspring* is singular and directly refers to Jesus Christ (Gal 3:16).

The New Testament begins with these words: *A record of the genealogy of Jesus Christ the son of David, the son of Abraham: (Matt 1:1).* This passage identifies Jesus Christ as the son of Abraham, the *offspring* through whom all the nations will be blessed. Obviously, Jesus Christ is not the divine son of Abraham, but the One who is descended physically from Abraham. Further, God identifies the importance of obedience. Abraham's obedience is the reason that the gospel is announced through him. In addition, the word, *blessed*, is synonymous with *justified*, which means pardoned, declared innocent, and set free. Christ is the basis of our justification that brings redemption and reconciliation with God.

God, acting through Christ, is the Origin and Source of the gospel of Christ. In like manner, Christ is the Source of justification, leading to salvation and eternal life.

As the apostle Paul stated: Christ, on the cross, justified all mankind and thereby brought life (salvation) for all men. *Consequently, just as the result of one trespass was condemnation for all men, so also the result of one act of righteousness was justification that brings life [salvation] for all men. (Rom 5:18)*

Paul, in 2 Cor 4:4, refers to the gospel of Christ as *the gospel of the glory of Christ*.

2 Timothy 1:9-10 presents the character of the gospel, the purpose of the gospel, and the result, which are the power of the resurrection and eternal life. "*The gospel is the light shining in the darkness of this world, and the light brings salvation (life) and the promise of immortality, which is the power of the resurrection, giving*

eternal life to everyone who believes." The gospel is the light of God shining in the darkness; the gospel brings forgiveness, salvation, resurrection, and eternal life to everyone who believes.

These passages attest to the power and importance of the gospel of Christ to all people and all nations throughout history.

In Scripture, the title most commonly used for the gospel is the *gospel of Christ,* which is used 8 times: *Rom 15:19; I Cor 9:12; 2 Cor 2:12; 2 Cor 9:13; 2 Cor 10:14; Gal 1:7; Phil 1:27; I Thess 3:2.* In addition, other variations of this term, the *gospel of Christ,* are three other titles: the *gospel of His Son (Rom 1:9), the gospel of the glory of Christ (2 Cor 4:4), and the gospel of our Lord Jesus Christ (2 Thess 1:8).*

In addition, the Scripture has seven other titles for the gospel: *The Gospel of the Kingdom (Matt 24:14); The Gospel of God's grace (Acts 20:24); The Gospel of God (Rom 1:1); The Gospel of your salvation (Eph 1:13); The Gospel of Peace: (Eph 6:15); The glorious Gospel of the blessed God (1 Tim 1:11); The eternal Gospel (Rev 14:6).* However, the predominant title for the gospel is *the gospel of Christ;* therefore, the title, *the gospel of Christ,* will be used throughout this book.

But what is this gospel of Christ?

The gospel of Christ is *good news from God which brings great joy to all who hear and receive.* However, the Bible contains both good news and bad news; it has good news for the righteous; it has bad news for unrepentant and disobedient sinners.

In all respects, the *gospel of Christ* is the centerpiece of Scripture.

The *gospel of Christ* includes the truth announced to Abraham, the promise of the Holy Spirit, the new covenant (Jeremiah 31:31-34) for the forgiveness of sins, the Incarnation of Jesus Christ, the spiritual birth, the earthly ministry of Christ, the coming of the Holy Spirit, the Cross of Christ, the resurrection, the ascension of Christ, the second coming of Christ, the general resurrection, the Final Judgment, and the coming of a New Heaven and a New Earth, and the New Jerusalem.

Perhaps the greatest promise and the greatest good news is that Christ is coming soon (Rev 22:7, 12, and 20).

Behold, I am coming soon! Blessed is he who keeps the words of the prophecy in this book. (Rev 22:7)

Behold, I am coming soon! My reward is with me, and I will give to everyone according to what he has done. (Rev 22:12)

He who testifies to these things says, "Yes, I am coming soon." Amen. Come, Lord Jesus. The grace of the Lord Jesus be with God's people. Amen. (Rev 22:20-21)

We begin by recognizing that there is one gospel of Christ; however, there are multiple versions of this one true gospel. The first written gospel account is that presented in Paul's Epistle to the Galatians, which is also the first recorded book of the New Testament (about 49 AD). Paul wrote his Epistle to the Romans, his sixth epistle and his version of the gospel, in approximately 57 AD, approximately 8 years after the Epistle to the Galatians.

This Epistle to the Romans begins with this statement: *I [Paul] am not ashamed of the gospel, because it is the power of God for the salvation of everyone who believes: first for the Jew, then for the Gentile. For in the gospel a righteousness from God is revealed, a righteousness that is by faith from first to last, just as it is written: "The righteous will live by faith." (Rom 1:16-17)*

This epistle ends its gospel argument in chapter 8: beginning with 8:1 and ending with 8:31-39.

Therefore, there is now no condemnation for those who are in Christ Jesus, because through Christ Jesus the law of the Spirit of life set me free from the law of sin and death. (Rom 8:1-2)....

What, then, shall we say in response to this? If God is for us, who can be against us? He who did not spare his own Son, but gave him up for us all — how will he not also, along with him, graciously give us all things? Who will bring any charge against those whom God has chosen? It is God who justifies. Who is he that condemns? Christ Jesus, who died — more than that, who was raised to life — is at the right hand of God and is also interceding for us. Who shall separate us from the love of Christ? Shall trouble or hardship or persecution or famine or nakedness or danger or sword? As it is written:

"For your sake we face death all day long;

we are considered as sheep to be slaughtered."

No, in all these things we are more than conquerors through him who loved us. For I am convinced that neither death nor life, neither angels nor demons, neither the present nor the future, nor any powers, neither height nor depth, nor anything else in all creation, will be able to separate us from the love of God that is in Christ Jesus our Lord. (Rom 8:31-39)

The gospel can be viewed as a series of events in the past, the present and the future. In the past, God has sent His only begotten Son, Jesus Christ, to redeem mankind, enslaved by sin. By His grace, we are redeemed and reconciled to the God and Father of all. In the present, we have been given the gift of the Holy Spirit to lead us into all righteousness, which is the godly trust and confidence in God for all things. In the future, we have the promise of the resurrection and eternal life, as the righteous reward for faith and works, in response to the grace of God. So the gospel can be viewed in the following context:

The past: Redemption and Reconciliation.
The present: Righteousness through the gift of the Spirit.
The future: Resurrection and Eternal Live.
That is the good news, the gospel message.

However, consider the later versions of the gospel as found in Matthew, Mark, Luke, John, and Romans. Mark, which is considered to be Peter's version, was written about 65-70 AD. This was followed by Matthew (70-75 AD), Luke (78-83 AD), and John (95-115 AD). The gospels according to Matthew, Mark, and Luke are called the synoptic gospels because they emphasize more the historical record of the birth, life, death, resurrection, and ascension of Jesus Christ. In a different manner, the gospel according to John is both an historical and theological statement.

Further, the Scriptures present Jesus Christ, the Person of the gospel, as Man, Servant, King, and God.

Matthew: Behold the Man (Zechariah 6:12)

> *Zech 6:12, Tell him this is what the LORD Almighty says: 'Here is the man whose name is the Branch, and he will branch out from his place and build the temple of the LORD'*

Mark: Behold, my Servant (Isaiah 42:1)

> *Isa 42:1, Here is my servant, whom I [God] uphold, my chosen one in whom I delight; I will put my Spirit on him and he will bring justice to the nations.*

Luke: Behold, thy King (Zechariah 9:9)

> *Zech 9:9, Rejoice greatly, O Daughter of Zion! Shout, Daughter of Jerusalem! See, your king comes to you, righteous and having salvation, gentle and riding on a donkey, on a colt, the foal of a donkey.*

John: Behold, your God (Isaiah 40:1)

> *Isa 40:1, Comfort, comfort my people, says your God.*

Although each version is different, they are also similar. They all unite in declaring the gospel of Christ; each contributes in its own way to the message of God for the redemption and reconciliation of mankind, enslaved by sin.

Specifically, the gospel is the *good news* that presents a combination of events and circumstances: of God's people in slavery, of a deliverer, sent by and from God, who will bring about redemption and reconciliation with God. The rewards of this gospel are the gift of the Spirit, the hope and certainty of the resurrection and the promise of eternal life in the City of God.

We have already seen the result of the acceptance of the gospel as described by the apostle Paul in Romans 8. The result is that nothing *will be able to separate us from the love of God that is in Christ Jesus our Lord. (Rom 8:39)*

Consider some events which represent the gospel of Christ.

As an example, consider the deliverance of the Israelites from slavery in Egypt. This good news points directly to the Cross of Christ.

Therefore, say to the Israelites: 'I am the LORD, and I will bring you out from under the yoke of the Egyptians. I will free you from being slaves to them, and I will redeem you with an outstretched arm and with mighty acts of judgment. I will take you as my own people, and I will be your God. Then you will know that I am the LORD your God, who brought you out from under the yoke of the Egyptians. And I will bring you to the land I swore with uplifted hand to give to Abraham, to Isaac and to Jacob. I will give it to you as a possession. I am the LORD.' (Ex 6:6-8)

This amazing passage has these promises of redemption and reconciliation. *I will free you....I will redeem you....I will take you as my own people.... I will be your God...I will bring you to the land I swore with uplifted hand to give to Abraham, to Isaac and to Jacob. I will give it to you as a possession. I am the LORD.* In this passage, notice that God says: I will be *your* God, which defines a personal relationship of enormous magnitude.

The gospel has good news in which the hand of God is evident, which describes a *deliverance from* and *a promise to a life* far better. It has a deliverer, chosen by God; it includes a covenant statement which is ratified by the God-chosen and God-sent deliverer.

There are those who seek the redemption and reconciliation that comes through the Cross of Christ; however, it is equally true that many people deny the Cross and refuse the redemption offered by Christ.

Only the Cross of Christ can bring about redemption and reconciliation. Only the Cross of Christ can bring the godless to God's saving grace.

However, genuine repentance must precede redemption and reconciliation. In addition, repentance has two essential features: we must *turn away* from evil, and we must *turn towards* goodness and righteousness. Both must occur. If we have only turned from evil, repentance is incomplete. We must turn from the darkness into the light.

As the book of Job states, Christians must do two things: they must *shun evil;* they must *fear God (Job 28:28)*. In the Bible, to *fear God* means to have reverence for God and to have an undivided devotion to the things of God.

We come to Christ, not because of what He can do for us, but because of what He has already done for us. We come out of gratitude, out of thanksgiving and out of love for the love which He first showed us.

He who knew no sin became sin for us: Christ, the Righteousness of God gave us His righteousness.

God is sovereign and supreme; we are sinners.

As a result, a major gulf separates holy God and sinful man. So how does a holy God become united to a sinful man? The answer is the Cross of Christ. Christ on the Cross unites God and man. The gospel is the truth of God; the bridge is the Cross of Christ, which offers mankind forgiveness, redemption, and reconciliation with God.

However, this union can only occur when the gospel is preached.

How beautiful on the mountains are the feet of those who bring good news, who proclaim peace, who bring good tidings, who proclaim salvation, who say to Zion, "Your God reigns!" (Isa 52:7)

For there is no difference between Jew and Gentile — the same Lord is Lord of all and richly blesses all who call on him, for, "Everyone who calls on the name of the Lord will be saved." How, then, can they call on the one they have not believed in? And how can they believe in the one of whom they have not heard? And how can they hear without someone preaching to them? And how can they preach unless they are sent? As it is written, "How beautiful are the feet of those who bring good news!" (Rom 10:12-15)

How beautiful are the feet of those who bring good news!

We are to bring good news of redemption through the Cross; we are to be ambassadors for Christ.

Consider Christ's command, regarding our responsibilities to proclaim the gospel. We are the hands and the voice for God. We must speak; we must act.

Then Jesus came to them [the disciples] and said, "All authority in heaven and on earth has been given to me. Therefore go and make disciples of all nations, baptizing them in the name of the Father and of the Son and of the Holy Spirit, and teaching them to obey everything I have commanded you. And surely I am with you always, to the very end of the age." (Matt 28:18-20)

But you will receive power when the Holy Spirit comes on you; and you will be my witnesses in Jerusalem, and in all Judea and Samaria, and to the ends of the earth." (Acts 1:8)

The gospel points to Christ on the Cross; the gospel proceeds from Christ on the Cross.

Christ on the Cross is the centerpiece of the gospel.

To accept Christ is to accept the gospel; to accept the gospel is to accept Christ. Christ and His gospel are inseparable.

God's love for the sinner is everlasting; God's desire for the salvation of the sinner is everlasting.

It is God's perfect patience that no one should perish (2 Peter 3:9).

The Lord is not slow in keeping his promise, as some understand slowness. He is patient with you, not wanting anyone to perish, but everyone to come to repentance. (2 Peter 3:9)

God's purpose in the gospel is to reestablish His relationship with sinful mankind. So how does God reestablish that relationship?

The answer is clear: *For God so loved the world that he gave his one and only Son, that whoever believes in him shall not perish but have eternal life. For God did not send his Son into the world to condemn the world, but to save the world through him. Whoever believes in him is not condemned, but whoever does not believe stands condemned already because he has not believed in the name of God's one and only Son. This is the verdict: Light has come into the world, but men loved darkness instead of light because their deeds were evil. Everyone who does evil hates the light, and will not come into the light for fear that his deeds will be exposed. But whoever lives by the truth comes into the light, so that it may be seen plainly that what he has done has been done through God. (John 3:16-21)*

God sent His Son to die for the sins of the world and to save the world through Him. God loved and He gave; He didn't give without loving; He didn't love without giving. Because of love, God sent His Son.

So the heart of the gospel is *Christ on the Cross.*

The cross is the bridge by which God reclaimed the hearts and the minds and the souls of sinners.

God is love, but God is a God of wrath. His wrath has always been directed at the godlessness and wickedness of men. God will not accept sinful conduct. God will not accept disobedience. His wrath is real and, in His holiness, evil will be dealt with. No one is immune from the wrath of God: there are divine consequences to sin.

God's love is real; God's wrath is real.

His love brings peace and joy and blessing; His wrath brings warning and punishment.

Christ demands love, dedication, commitment, sacrifice, unselfishness, faithfulness, and peace. In exchange, Christ offers God's love, God's protection, God's provision, the resurrection, and eternal life in the City of God.

This book is centered on that gospel, fully associated with Jesus Christ, who is Savior and Lord, who is the Son of God, who is God the Son, who is the Word made flesh, who is the Light of the world, who is the Resurrection and the Life, who is the Way, the Truth, and the Life, who is the Bread of Life, who is the Good Shepherd, who is the True Vine, who is the Author and Perfecter of our Faith, who is our Great High Priest, who is the Lamb of God, who is the Perfect Sacrifice for the sins of the world, who is the Fullness of Righteousness, and the One in whom the fullness of the deity was pleased to dwell. He is the image of the invisible God; He is the firstborn of all creation. All things were created by Him and for Him. He is the One through whom all are redeemed and reconciled to God, by making peace through His blood, shed on the Cross.

Unfortunately, the gospel of Christ is one of the most neglected doctrines of Christianity. As a result, evangelism wanes.

The gospel is not proclaimed with faithfulness, commitment, and regularity. The church may not proclaim the gospel because it doesn't know the gospel. It may not know the gospel because it doesn't teach the gospel. It doesn't teach the gospel because it may be unfaithful in serving Christ as Head of the Church and as Savior and Lord.

The gospel is a message of love: there is no greater message for the church to proclaim and teach.

It is a message for those who know the *absence of love*; it is a message for those who know the *presence of sin*.

It is possible that those who seek God will be found by Him; we need to help the world in that search.

So we approach this wonderful subject, the *gospel of Christ*.

In doing so, we shall begin by examining: first, four doctrines that establish the *theology of the gospel*; second, we shall look at the *purpose of the gospel*; third, we shall study the *definition of the gospel* as contained in the Epistle to the Romans; fourth, we shall study the *message of the gospel;* fifth, we shall look at the results of *decision* regarding the gospel; sixth, we shall examine our *Christian responsibility* regarding the gospel; seventh, we shall look at the *spiritual warfare* which we face in proclaiming the gospel. Finally, we shall acknowledge the *victory that we have in Christ.*

Then I heard what sounded like a great multitude, like the roar of rushing waters and like loud peals of thunder, shouting: "Hallelujah! For our Lord God Almighty reigns. Let us rejoice and be glad and give him glory! (Rev 19:6-7)

So, as a prelude to the gospel of Christ, we begin by a discussion of the theology of the gospel.

Primary to that theology is the *Sovereignty* of God. His sovereignty is the basis of His authority. That is the foundation upon which all of Scripture and all of life is based.

Second, we address *The Love of God* which is the primary expression of His sovereignty and authority.

Third, we address *The Cross of Christ* which is the ultimate expression of the love of God.

Fourth, we address *The Power of the Holy Spirit* whom God has sent to equip His people to proclaim the gospel and advance the kingdom.

The gospel of Christ is based on the truths contained in these four doctrines.

We now address the *Sovereignty of God*.

PART 1

The Theology of the Gospel

Chapter 2

The Sovereignty of God

In the beginning God created the heavens and the earth. (Gen 1:1)

See, the Sovereign LORD comes with power, and his arm rules for him. See, his reward is with him, and his recompense accompanies him. (Isa 40:10)

Then the sovereignty, power and greatness of the kingdoms under the whole heaven will be handed over to the saints, the people of the Most High. His kingdom will be an everlasting kingdom, and all rulers will worship and obey him. (Dan 7:27)

The sovereignty of God is the foundation for all of creation, for the love of God, for the word of God, for the redemption and reconciliation of sinners, for salvation, for eternal life, for truth, and for faith in God.

There is nothing that exists, except by the sovereignty of God.

Consider the passages at the beginning of this chapter.

Genesis 1:1 states: *in the beginning God....*There is no beginning aside from that begun by God.

Isaiah 40:10 states that God is the One of power and authority.

Daniel 7:27 confirms that God's kingdom will be an everlasting kingdom.

God is revealed fully as sovereign and with all authority. From these two designations, sovereignty and authority, flow all of His divine attributes: His power, His love, His wrath, His holiness, His righteousness, His justice, and His will for redemption and reconciliation.

Certainly, in addition to accepting His sovereignty and authority, we must honor God as love (I John 4:8) and God as Spirit (John 4:24).

This is how we should see the Living God. In one way, we should see the living God as Job saw Him. We should see the living God as Paul saw Him. It is an awesome thing to encounter the Living God, and yet that is what we are to do.

The sovereignty of God also establishes the authority of Christ and that of the Holy Spirit. In addition, the authority of God is the foundation for the authority of the word of God; it follows that the authority of the word of God is the foundation for the authority of the gospel.

To understand the Bible in general and the gospel in particular, we must first understand the sovereignty and authority of God. In a theological sense, *sovereign* means to be before all others, to be supreme in all power in all places at all times, to be superior to all others in every situation, to be independent of others and unlimited by others.

There is no time in which God has not been sovereign; there is no place, in heaven and on earth, in which God has not been sovereign. God Himself, Jesus Christ, the Holy Spirit, the Bible, the Old Testament patriarchs, and the New Testament apostles, all attest to God as sovereign.

The title, *sovereign*, is used 298 times in combination with the word *Lord* in the Old Testament, and 5 times in the New Testament. God is eternally recognized and referred to as the *Sovereign Lord* beginning with Abraham (Gen 15:2) and concluding with *"the souls of those who had been slain because of the word of God and the testimony they had maintained. They called out in a loud voice, 'How long, Sovereign Lord, holy and true, until you judge the inhabitants of the earth and avenge our blood?'" (Rev 6:9-10)*

We should see Him as Sovereign Lord: that is the reason we love Him; that is the reason that we obey Him; that is the reason we serve Him; that is the reason we worship Him.

As sovereign, the authority of God is measured primarily by His acts of creation and redemption. As sovereign, He is the One against whom all laws, principles, values, and standards are measured. He is sovereign in His justice, which is loving and eminently fair and equitable. As Lawgiver and Judge, He is the standard for both. As sovereign, He determines the quality of all lives; He governs all that occurs. As sovereign, He is the Author of Life, the Giver of liberty and freedom, the Source of all power. As sovereign, He is the Love against which all love, both divine and human, is measured. As sovereign, His plan for His creation is perfect; His plan will be fulfilled. As sovereign, His will for His people is perfect. His will is that we should live a life worthy of our calling as children of God, that we should know the fullness of His salvation, and that we would eventually share eternity with Him.

King David attests to the sovereignty of God: *How great you are, O Sovereign LORD! There is no one like you, and there is no God but you, as we have heard with our own ears. (2 Sam 7:22)*

In like manner, the apostle Paul wrote to his friend, Timothy. *Now to the King eternal, immortal, invisible, the only God, be honor and glory forever and ever. Amen. (1 Tim 1:17)*

Divine sovereignty and divine authority represent a divine right and a moral right.

His sovereignty is the foundation of both His divine authority and His divine power. In like manner, Jesus Christ had both authority and power (Luke 4:36; Matthew 28:18); further, Christ bestowed these upon His followers (Luke 10:19).

Relative to sovereignty, God has *authority* which is unlimited and unrestrained.

He has *authority* to initiate and the authority to produce. He has authority to set standards for the world; He instructs the world;

He can demand performance; He can judge results, consistent with His authority. No one can question or deny His authority; it is the ultimate absolute.

Further, we believe in God's sovereignty and authority because we believe in Christ. Conversely, our faith in Christ is the basis of our faith in God. *Through Christ, you believe in God.* That is the truth of I Peter 1:20-21.

Through him [Christ] you believe in God, who raised him from the dead and glorified him, and so your faith and hope are in God. (1 Peter 1:20-21)

Now, the authority of God is the foundation for all other authority, divine and secular.

Everyone must submit himself to the governing authorities, for there is no authority except that which God has established. The authorities that exist have been established by God. (Rom 13:1)

In addition, His sovereignty and authority are the basis of the gospel. We believe in the gospel, because we believe in the sovereignty and authority of God, who is the Origin and Source of the gospel.

God has sent forth two Words, His living Word, Jesus Christ, and His written word, the Bible. God has all authority; His Word has all authority; His gospel has all authority. These two *Words*, Jesus Christ, the Living Word, and the Bible, the written Word, attest to the sovereignty and authority of God.

His written word and His living Word, Jesus, the Christ, unite to provide the basis of our relationship with God. *In the beginning was the Word, and the Word was with God, and the Word was God. He was with God in the beginning. (John 1:1-2)*

In this passage, the *Word was God* was from the beginning and through Him, the Living Word, were all things made. The Word gives light, which penetrates and shines in the darkness. Here is another purpose for the Word of God, which is to bring light (i.e. God's truth) into an otherwise dark and evil world.

The apostle Paul understood the power and authority of the written word, which he summarized in 2 Timothy 3:14-17: *But as for you [Timothy], continue in what you have learned and have firmly believed, knowing from whom you learned it and how from childhood you have been acquainted with the sacred writings which are able to instruct you for salvation through faith in Christ Jesus. All scripture is inspired by God and profitable for teaching, for reproof, for correction, and for training in righteousness, that the man of God may be complete, equipped for every good work.*

In that passage, Paul identified the *objective* of Scripture, the *origin* of Scripture, the *profitability* or value of Scripture, and the *purpose* of Scripture.

The objective of Scripture is *to instruct you for salvation through faith in Christ Jesus.*

The origin of Scripture is by the inspiration of God which means by the breath of God. God *breathed*, and His word came forth, in much the same way as God spoke and creation came into being. The Breath of God, His Holy Spirit, leads to Creation and to the word of God.

Next, the profitability or value of Scripture resides in four areas: it is *profitable for teaching, for reproof, for correction, and for training in righteousness.*

Finally, Paul identifies the purpose of Scripture: *that the man of God may be complete, equipped for every good work.*

Further, the authority of the written word is because the Holy Spirit is the *Author* of that word. He is the same *Author* and the same inspiration for the gospel of Christ. The word of God must be accepted as divine and worthy of eternal honor, respect, and acceptance. *For prophecy never had its origin in the will of man, but men spoke from God as they were carried along by the Holy Spirit. (2 Peter 1:20)*

Men spoke from God; this is an essential element of divine disclosure and human acceptance of the Word of God revealed to men. For example, in the Old Testament, there are 262 times when the phrase, *the word of the Lord*, came to men. This expression is first revealed in Genesis 15:1 with Abram. It is amazing that the term is found 68 times in Jeremiah and 62 times in Ezekiel.

In addition, the *word of the Lord* also came to Moses, to Samuel, to Nathan, to David, to Solomon, to Jehu, to Elijah, to Elisha, to Isaiah, to Jeremiah, to Ezekiel, to Haggia, and to Zechariah and to almost every prophet. The Old Testament is a witness to the fact that God spoke to men for their instruction, for their confidence in God, and as a warning against the consequences of evil and wickedness.

In this written word, the Sovereign God has given the world a great mystery, which is the presence of Christ is us.

To them God has chosen to make known among the Gentiles the glorious riches of this mystery, which is Christ in you, the hope of glory. (Col 1:27)

The ultimate *hope* of all Christians is *glory*, which is the divine completion of salvation. When understood in this context, Christian *hope* is *the certainty of glory.*

From the authority of the Bible, we now turn to the authority of the gospel.

The truth is this: the gospel has authority because it is founded on the sovereignty and authority of God and the authority of His word. To accept one is to accept the others.

The full representation of the gospel is revealed in the Person of Christ. If Christ is accepted as Savior and Lord, then His gospel must be accepted. Conversely, if His gospel is accepted, then His Person must be accepted.

Christ and His gospel are inseparable.

The gospel is the message of salvation; the salvation that comes through Christ can be described as past, present, and future. When a person believes in Christ, he is saved (Acts 16:31). But we are also in the process of daily being saved from the power of sin (Rom 8:13; Phil 2:12). Ultimately, in the future, we shall be fully freed from the power of sin (Rom 13:11; Titus 2:12-13). Our salvation will be completed when Christ returns (Heb 9:28) and the kingdom of God is fully revealed (Matt 13:41-43).

Salvation has the dimension of being justified, edified, sanctified, and glorified.

Salvation, begun in justification, will be completed in glorification.

The principal characteristic of the Sovereign Lord is love; that is the subject we now address.

Chapter 3

The Love of God

For great is your love, higher than the heavens; your faithfulness reaches to the skies. Be exalted, O God, above the heavens, and let your glory be over all the earth. (Psa 108:4-5)

The earth is filled with your love, O LORD; (Psa 119:64)

A new command I [Christ] give you: Love one another. As I have loved you, so you must love one another. By this all men will know that you are my disciples, if you love one another. (John 13:34-35)

And so we know and rely on the love God has for us. God is love. Whoever lives in love lives in God, and God in him. (1 John 4:16)

The foundation of the Bible is the sovereignty of God; His sovereignty is best expressed in His love. In like manner, the foundation of the gospel is the love of God.

The gospel is the ultimate expression of the love of God.

The first passage, Psalm 108:4-5, describes the love of God as an expression of His faithfulness and the reflection of His glory.

Psalm 119:64 states that God's creation is filled with His love.

John 13:34 states the character of the new command from Christ: we are to love as He has loved us. He is the example of love: He is the expression and witness of the love of God.

The passage, I John 4:16, identifies God as love; that is His name.

At the same time, God is a God of wrath (Rom 1:18): His wrath is revealed from heaven against all evil and wickedness. He is a holy God who cannot and will not abide sin. The wrath of God is mentioned 197 times in Scripture, and there are 10 specific references in the Book of Revelation.

His love is real; His wrath is real.

His love is to bless, encourage, and reward; His wrath is to warn and to punish.

His love cannot be defined, but there are examples, evidence, and expressions of His love.

However, love is the divine keystone of God: it is the basis and foundation of His omnipotence, His omniscience, and His omnipresence. In addition, love is central to the character of Jesus, the Christ. The Holy Spirit, the Spirit of Truth, will lead us into all truth, which includes the understanding, appreciation, and acceptance of the love of God.

Love has two basic dimensions: *grace* and *mercy*.

Grace is God giving us His love, which we do not deserve. Conversely, *mercy* is God *not* giving us His wrath, what we do deserve. Grace bestows love; mercy withholds wrath.

But love is also intimately involved with truth. Truth and love are inseparably connected. Where there is truth, there is and will be love. Where there is love, there is and will be truth.

It is true that divine love reflects the fullness of the truth about God. God is truth; in one way that statement is the foundation that God is love. Because God is truth, we can believe and have confidence that God is love.

One of the reasons that Jesus Christ came into the world was to testify to the truth, which is that God is love. In John 18:37, *Jesus answered, "You [Pilate] are right in saying I am a king. In fact, for this reason I was born, and for this I came into the world, to testify to the truth."*

In Christ's great priestly prayer (John 17), Jesus prayed for the protection of His followers and for our unity, in the same manner that the Father and the Son are one: *so that they may be one as we are one. (John 17:11)*

God is love, and He is also truth.

Consider the many passages in Scripture describing and defining that God is the God of truth. Not only is God the God of truth (Psa 31:5), everything coming from God is truth. Therefore, the Bible is the book of truth (Dan 10:21); the truth of God will guide us to the dwelling place of God (Psa 43:3); Jerusalem, the holy city, is called the City of Truth (Zech 8:3); divine truth is the basis of our freedom in Christ (John 8:31); the Holy Spirit, the Spirit of Truth, will lead believers into all truth (John 16:13); Jesus came into the world to testify to the truth (John 18:37); love rejoices in the truth (I Cor 13:6); the word of truth is the gospel of our salvation (Eph 1:13).

Consider a few passages dealing with God as Truth.

Into your hands I commit my spirit; redeem me, O LORD, the God of truth. (Psa 31:5)

Send forth your light and your truth, let them guide me; let them bring me to your holy mountain, to the place where you dwell. (Ps 43:3)

but first I will tell you what is written in the Book of Truth. (Dan 10:21)

This is what the LORD says: "I will return to Zion and dwell in Jerusalem. Then Jerusalem will be called the City of Truth, and the mountain of the LORD Almighty will be called the Holy Mountain." (Zech 8:3)

But when he, the Spirit of truth, comes, he will guide you into all truth. (John 16:13)

Sanctify them by the truth; your word is truth. (John 17:17)

Love does not delight in evil but rejoices with the truth. (1 Cor 13:6)

And you also were included in Christ when you heard the word of truth, the gospel of your salvation. Having believed, you were marked in him with a seal, the promised Holy Spirit, who is a deposit guaranteeing our inheritance until the redemption of those who are God's possession — to the praise of his glory. (Eph 1:13-14)

The word of God, the God of truth, is the gospel of our salvation.

God is love; God is truth. Love is the evidence of truth as truth is the evidence of love.

The Gospel of John contains this passage: *For the law was given through Moses; grace and truth came through Jesus Christ. (John 1:17).*

Here we have the relationship between the law, grace and truth.

The law, given through Moses, was given to reveal sin.

Grace and truth came through Jesus Christ.

It is also true that grace, mercy, and truth are three aspects of the love of God. Grace is love undeserved; mercy is wrath withheld; truth is love revealed. There is no greater truth than that God is love. To know the truth is to know love; to know love is to know the truth. Christ is the Truth; Christ is love.

The gospel message is the message of the love of God.

We acknowledge that there are two types of love: human and divine.

In addition, there are four relevant Greek words which describe human love: *stergo* (love within the family), *philia* (friendship between people), *eros* (sensual or erotic love), and *philadelphia* (love among brothers who are not related).

However, there is one Greek word for *love* which transcends all secular definitions; that word is *agape*, which is the divine love that defines God's relationship with His people and with His creation.

This type of spiritual love takes our lives and everything around us to a greater height and to a greater depth than any other experience in life. The reason that this is true is because spiritual love involves the God who created us and His universe. God is present and involved in *agape*.

In this discussion of the love of God, it is important to realize that to define love is to define God. Such a definition is impossible for the human mind. The apostle Paul grappled with this issue. Paul wrote that he could describe love, but he couldn't define it (I Corinthians 13).

The love of God is because of the mind and will of God. But who can know fully either the mind of God or the will of God? It is beyond human comprehension. In like manner, it is equally presumptuous to claim to know and understand fully the love of God.

However, God has revealed His love in His word and through His Son. Therefore, God has given us specific revelations of His love, which enables us to understand the character of love that God demonstrates and which He envisions for His children.

If we want to understand the love of God, then we have only to look to the Cross of Christ. Two truths come thundering in on me.

First, I am confronted with the seriousness of my sin; for me to realize that my sin is so great that only God could pay the price to redeem so great a sinner. From the perspective of the cross, I can never take sin lightly; its price exceeds any human understanding. It is love beyond understanding.

Second, I experience God's enormous love for sinners. I am amazed: that a pure and holy and righteous and just God loves me so much that He gave His only begotten Son that whosoever believed in Him would not perish but have eternal life.

The cross is a witness to the truth that while we were yet sinners, Christ died for us. The cross is a witness to the enormous love of God for sinners.

The Cross of Christ completely defines the love of God.

God is love (I John 4:16): that remarkable statement defies comprehension.

However, that statement is the basis of His creation; it is the basis of His relationship with His created; it is the basis of His promises; it is the basis of His commandments; it is the basis of our redemption and reconciliation; it is the basis of eternity for all who love and serve Him.

God and love are synonymous.

We recognize the supreme love of God, expressed in the incarnation, the baptism, the crucifixion, the resurrection, and the ascension of Jesus Christ.

God's love is expressed in Christ's ministry and purpose for coming into the world. Here is expressed the divine love through the gift of the Son of God. God loved but He also gave; He did not love without giving, and His gift of His Son for the sins of the world is the most complete and fundamental expression of His love for the world.

For God so loved the world that he gave his one and only Son, that whoever believes in him shall not perish but have eternal life. For God did not send his Son into the world to condemn the world, but to save the world through him. Whoever believes in him is not condemned, but whoever does not believe stands condemned already because he has not believed in the name of God's one and only Son. This is the verdict: Light has come into the world, but men loved darkness instead of light because their deeds were evil. Everyone who does evil hates the light, and will not come into the light for fear that his deeds will be exposed. But whoever lives by the truth comes into the light, so that it may be seen plainly that what he has done has been done through God. (John 3:16-21)

The love of God is expressed in the birth, life, death, resurrection, and ascension of Jesus Christ, so that all who believe in Him would not perish but have eternal life. God sent His Son into the world to save the world. To accomplish that, Christ was the Light that came into the world, so that those who lived in darkness might come into the light. The love of God is evident and visible in every aspect of the life and ministry of Christ.

Therefore, the dominant word of the Bible is love; in like manner, the dominant word of the gospel is love. The love of God leads to this result: we have peace with God. Peace is the divine unity that Christ spoke of in John 17.

The Scriptures reveal the love of God. So let us examine some of the passages in Scripture which express this agape love.

Hear, O Israel: The LORD our God, the LORD is one. Love the LORD your God with all your heart and with all your soul and with all your strength. These commandments that I [Moses] give you today are to be upon your hearts. Impress them on your children. Talk about them when you sit at home and when you walk along the road, when you lie down and when you get up. *(Deut 6:4-8)*

O LORD, God of Israel, there is no God like you in heaven or on earth — you who keep your covenant of love with your servants who continue wholeheartedly in your way. *(2 Chron 6:14)*

Surely goodness and love will follow me all the days of my life, and I will dwell in the house of the LORD forever. *(Ps 23:6)*

For the LORD is good and his love endures forever; his faithfulness continues through all generations. *(Ps 100:5)*

May your unfailing love come to me, O LORD, your salvation according to your promise; *(Ps 119:41)*

And a voice from heaven said, "This is my Son, whom I love; with him I am well pleased." *(Matt 3:17)*

For God so loved the world that he gave his one and only Son, that whoever believes in him shall not perish but have eternal life. For God did not send his Son into the world to condemn the world, but to save the world through him. *(John 3:16-17)*

My [Christ] command is this: Love each other as I have loved you. *(John 15:12-13)*

But God demonstrates his own love for us in this: While we were still sinners, Christ died for us. *(Rom 5:8)*

And we know that in all things God works for the good of those who love him, who have been called according to his purpose. *(Rom 8:28)*

But the fruit of the Spirit is love, joy, peace, patience, kindness, goodness, faithfulness, gentleness and self-control. Against such things there is no law. *(Gal 5:22-23)*

For he chose us in him before the creation of the world to be holy and blameless in his sight. In love he predestined us to be adopted as his sons through Jesus Christ, in accordance with his pleasure and will— to the praise of his glorious grace, which he has freely given us in the One he loves. *(Eph 1:4-6)*

But because of his great love for us, God, who is rich in mercy, made us alive with Christ even when we were dead in transgressions — it is by grace you have been saved. *(Eph 2:4-6)*

My purpose is that they may be encouraged in heart and united in love, so that they may have the full riches of complete understanding, in order that they may know the mystery of God, namely, Christ, in whom are hidden all the treasures of wisdom and knowledge. (Col 2:2-4)

How great is the love the Father has lavished on us, that we should be called children of God! And that is what we are! The reason the world does not know us is that it did not know him. (1 John 3:1)

Whoever does not love does not know God, because God is love. This is how God showed his love among us: He sent his one and only Son into the world that we might live through him. This is love: not that we loved God, but that he loved us and sent his Son as an atoning sacrifice for our sins. (1 John 4:8-11)

No one has ever seen God; but if we love one another, God lives in us and his love is made complete in us. (1 John 4:12)

If anyone acknowledges that Jesus is the Son of God, God lives in him and he in God. And so we know and rely on the love God has for us. God is love. Whoever lives in love lives in God, and God in him. In this way, love is made complete among us so that we will have confidence on the day of judgment, because in this world we are like him. There is no fear in love. But perfect love drives out fear, because fear has to do with punishment. The one who fears is not made perfect in love. We love because he first loved us. If anyone says, "I love God," yet hates his brother, he is a liar. For anyone who does not love his brother, whom he has seen, cannot love God, whom he has not seen. And he has given us this command: Whoever loves God must also love his brother. (1 John 4:15-21)

God is love; that is the ultimate divine truth. It is the Truth of truths.

We now turn to the fullness of the expression of the love of God: The Cross of Christ.

Chapter 4

The Cross of Christ

This man [Jesus Christ] was handed over to you by God's set purpose and foreknowledge; and you, with the help of wicked men, put him to death by nailing him to the cross. But God raised him from the dead, freeing him from the agony of death, because it was impossible for death to keep its hold on him. (Acts 2:23-25)

For Christ did not send me [Paul] to baptize, but to preach the gospel — not with words of human wisdom, lest the cross of Christ be emptied of its power. For the message of the cross is foolishness to those who are perishing, but to us who are being saved it is the power of God. (1 Cor 1:17-18)

I [Paul] have been crucified with Christ and I no longer live, but Christ lives in me. The life I live in the body, I live by faith in the Son of God, who loved me and gave himself for me. (Gal 2:20)

He forgave us all our sins, having canceled the written code, with its regulations, that was against us and that stood opposed to us; he took it away, nailing it to the cross. And having disarmed the powers and authorities, he made a public spectacle of them, triumphing over them by the cross. (Col 2:13-15)

We now address *The Cross of Christ* as the third doctrine essential to the gospel of Christ. This subject identifies the Person of the gospel and the heart of the gospel.

The passages at the beginning of this section present major truths regarding the Cross of Christ.

The first passage, Acts 2:23-25, presents the truth that the Cross was no accident nor was it the plan of men. Luke presents this truth: that the Cross was according to *God's set purpose and foreknowledge.* The Cross was the plan of God for the forgiveness of sins and the redemption of mankind.

In I Corinthian 1:17-18, the Cross defines the power of God.

In Galatians 2:20, Paul stated that Christ lived in him because Paul had been crucified with Christ.

In Colossians 2:13-15, our sins were nailed to the cross; and, by the cross, we have victory through the cross.

The Cross of Christ is the ultimate defining moment in divine and secular history. Christ, the Son of God, is the supreme and ultimate Witness to God the Father, to Creation, and to the existence of mankind.

The Cross of Christ is the defining reason for which God sent His Son into the world. Christ set His face directly to the Cross, to die for the sins of the world and to make us the righteousness of God.

The Cross of Christ identifies the basis of the forgiveness of sin, of redemption, of reconciliation, of the gift of the Spirit, of the basis of salvation, of the resurrection, and the certainty of eternal life.

However, there is little possibility that we will ever understand the full significance of the Cross of Christ.

To understand the cross and all its implications, we would have to have been there for the trials before Caiaphas and Pilate, for the scourging, for the crowd demanding His crucifixion, for the agonizing sight of Christ carrying His cross, for the hammers slamming the nails into His flesh, for the passion and agony of the Son of God, for the cries of Christ to the Father, for the two prisoners on either side, for those who ridiculed Him, for those who mocked and cast contempt on Christ, for the presence of His mother and the apostle John watching the whole event.

Everyone can imagine the physical agony, but no one can ever imagine the spiritual agony of the separation of the Son from the Father. That separation was the ultimate agony.

This much is certain: the Cross of Christ is the heart of the gospel of God. The cross is the heart of the Bible. Christ on the Cross, dying for the sins of the world, is the ultimate moment in all of divine and secular history. For that reason, we must make every effort to understand the Cross of Christ.

We cannot separate Christ from His Cross.

During His earthly ministry, He set His face steadfastly for Jerusalem, knowing the will of His Father and knowing what lay ahead of Him.

Christ on the cross is the supreme example of the love of God.

To understand the cross is to understand love.

In addition, Christ on the Cross is the Light who came into the world to reveal the truth.

For God so loved the world that he gave his one and only Son, that whoever believes in him shall not perish but have eternal life. For God did not send his Son into the world to condemn the world, but to save the world through him. Whoever believes in him is not condemned, but whoever does not believe stands condemned already because he has not believed in the name of God's one and only Son. This is the verdict: Light has come into the world, but men loved darkness instead of light because their deeds were evil. Everyone who does evil hates the light, and will not come into the light for fear that his deeds will be exposed. But whoever lives by the truth comes into the light, so that it may be seen plainly that what he has done has been done through God. (John 3:16-21)

This passage revealed His reason for being sent into the world, but it also identified the manner of His death and the purpose of His death. His manner: He would be lifted up (crucified): the purpose: so that all who believed in Him would have eternal life. This is in fulfillment of that foreshadowed by Moses in the wilderness.

I have spoken to you of earthly things and you do not believe; how then will you believe if I speak of heavenly things? No one has ever gone into heaven except the one who came from heaven — the Son of Man. Just as Moses lifted up the snake in the desert, so the Son of Man must be lifted up, that everyone who believes in him may have eternal life. (John 3:12-15)

For the world enslaved by sin, Jesus Christ is the Deliverer and the Savior of the world. That is the purpose for which He came into the world.

The cross was God's instrument to rescue us from this present evil age (Gal 1:4). This cross, this most hated symbol of punishment and suffering, was the fate of the Suffering Servant, Christ our Lord.

However, the Cross of Christ was foreshadowed in the Old Testament by four events: the Flood, the Exodus, the new covenant, and the sin sacrifice ordained by God. Each of these warrants our attention.

First, The Flood and the Cross:

The Flood represented God's judgment on the wickedness of all people, and it was the manner in which God initially dealt with sin.

The LORD saw how great man's wickedness on the earth had become, and that every inclination of the thoughts of his heart was only evil all the time. The LORD was grieved that he had made man on the earth, and his heart was filled with pain. So the LORD said, "I will wipe mankind, whom I have created, from the face of the earth — men and animals, and creatures that move along the ground, and birds of the air — for I am grieved that I have made them." (Gen 6:5-8)

Here is recorded wickedness and evil: here is recorded that *The LORD was grieved that he had made man on the earth, and his heart was filled with pain.* Can anyone imagine the Creator of the Universe being grieved and His heart filled with pain! So God determined *to bring floodwaters on the earth to destroy all life under the heavens.*

God's answer to sin was the destruction of all that was the source of sin. However, God resolved never again to destroy all life.

So, for the repentant sinner, God determined to solve the issue of sin by a new covenant, whose primary provision would be for the forgiveness of sin. For such a divine ratification, God determined that the only suitable sacrificial Lamb would be His only-begotten Son on the cross.

In the New Testament, God dealt with sin in a different manner. When sin was confessed, and sinners repented, God determined to redeem them and reconcile them to Himself.

On the cross, a divine exchange took place. On the cross, the righteousness of the Son of God was exchanged for the sins of mankind.

We now move to the Exodus which also foreshadowed the cross.

Second, The Exodus and the Cross:

Consider the Exodus as it directs our attention to Christ on the cross. In the Exodus, God responded to the cries of His people in *physical* slavery to an evil Pharaoh. God chose a human *deliverer*, Moses, whom God sent to Egypt to free His people. God demonstrated, through Moses, His love, His protection, and His provision. God not only set them free from Egypt, but He made provision for a better home and a better future. God ordained a physical kingdom under His love, His rule, and His authority.

The Exodus, a physical event, demonstrated the love and the power of God. God was their Savior.

Next, consider the Cross of Christ. God's people were in *spiritual* slavery to sin: now, God sent another *Deliverer,* His only begotten Son, Jesus Christ, to free His people and to lead them to the Promised Land, which is eternal life in the Kingdom of God.

Therefore, the cross is both a physical and a spiritual event, with Christ as our Deliverer.

Next, let us turn to the witness of the sin sacrifice.

Third, The Sin Sacrifice

The sin offering also directly foreshadows the cross. In essence, an offering or sacrifice has three central ideas: consecration, expiation (covering of sin), and propitiation (satisfaction of divine anger).

Both the Old Testament and the New Testament confirm that sacrifices were presented as a symbolic gesture. Man was obligated, because of his sin, to present offerings by which he gave another life in place of his own. Ultimately, such sacrifices lead to the one final and perfect sacrifice of Jesus Christ (Heb 10:11-18).

According to God's command, the animal sacrificed had to be physically perfect; and, through the perfection of this animal, perfection was presented to God. Ultimately, this symbolized the necessity for man to present himself perfect before God by presenting the perfect one in his place (1 Peter 1:18-19). The true Lamb of God, innocent of all sin, took away sin (John 1:29).

After the animal was selected and presented at the altar, the first act was the laying on of hands by the person presenting the offering. By this act, the worshiper symbolically transferred his sin and guilt to the sacrificial animal which stood in his place. The sacrifice symbolically pointed to Jesus Christ who would do for the believer what he could not do for himself. He would take upon Himself sin and guilt and accomplish redemption for His people (Isa 53:4-12; Matt 1:21).

We now turn to the final foreshadowed event, the new covenant.

Fourth, The New Covenant (Jer 31:31-34)

The fourth event that foreshadowed the cross was the new covenant, prophesized through Jeremiah, with its five promises: *first, I [God] will put my law within them, and I will write it upon their hearts; second, I will be their God, and they shall be my people; third, they shall all know me, from the least of them to the greatest; fourth, I will forgive their iniquity; fifth, I will remember their sin no more.*

Six centuries after Jeremiah proclaimed this new covenant, Christ met with His disciples in an upper room in Jerusalem to celebrate the Passover meal. Since the time of the Exodus, the Passover meal was celebrated in recognition of God's protection and deliverance of the Israelites by God. It commemorated the sacrificial death of the Paschal or Passover lamb, which was the blood shed for their deliverance from physical slavery.

Also, approximately 1,500 years after the Exodus, the blood of that Passover lamb was to be the blood of Jesus Christ, the Lamb of God, who was both the physical and spiritual Paschal Lamb. Christ, the true Paschal Lamb, was to free and deliver repentant sinners from the sins of the world.

The next day John [the Baptist] saw Jesus coming toward him and said, "Look, the Lamb of God, who takes away the sin of the world! (John 1:29)

It was necessary to ratify this covenant which was accomplished on the Cross of Christ.

The author of Hebrews verified the importance of blood to ratify a covenant. *In fact, the law requires that nearly everything be cleansed with blood, and without the shedding of blood there is no forgiveness. (Heb 9:22)*

Closely associated with the Passover meal was the Feast of Unleavened Bread. The Passover related to blood: the companion feast relates to unleavened bread. The Passover referred to the sacrifice of a lamb, and the Israelites smeared the blood of the lamb on their doorposts so that the angel of death, sent by God, would *pass over* their houses when He destroyed the firstborn in Egypt. The Exodus contains both the Passover feast and the Feast of Unleavened Bread: the Passover was to signify protection; the Feast of Unleavened Bread was to signify provision.

Now, Christ became the true Paschal Lamb; Christ became the Bread of life.

The Exodus takes on a whole new meaning when the Cross of Christ comes on the scene.

By His cross, the Passover celebration would be given a new and far greater significance. That night, when Jesus Christ met with His disciples in that upper room in Jerusalem, the Passover was dramatically and eternally changed. To understand the significance of that change, consider Christ's words that evening.

While they were eating, Jesus took bread, gave thanks and broke it, and gave it to his disciples, saying, "Take and eat; this is my body." Then he took the cup, gave thanks and offered it to them, saying, "Drink from it, all of you. This is my blood of the [new] covenant, which is poured out for many for the forgiveness of sins. I tell you, I will not drink of this fruit of the vine from now on until that day when I drink it anew with you in my Father's kingdom." (Matt 26:26-29)

Christ said that the bread was my body; Christ said that the wine was my blood of the new covenant which is poured out for many for the forgiveness of sin.

The blood of Christ, shed on the cross, ratified the new covenant which God proclaimed through Jeremiah six centuries earlier.

This covenant message is what Christians celebrate today as the Eucharist or Holy Communion. Its two principal promises are the forgiveness of sin and that these sins, confessed and repented, will be remembered no more.

The Passover provided *divine protection*; the Feast of Unleavened Bread ensured *divine provision*.

And there are many Old Testament events which foreshadow the Cross of Christ.

The cross is a supreme example of power consistent with all the acts of Creation. Consider the following: God, in both His divinity and in human form and flesh, was on the cross. The humanity, present in Christ, died on the Cross; physical death did not invade the immortal Spirit of the immortal God. Believe it. Further, the divinity, present in Christ, exchanged His divine righteousness for the sins of the world. The divine Christ became sin so that man could become the righteousness of God. The humanity, present in Christ, was dead and buried. However, the humanity, present in Christ, was raised from the dead, fulfilling God's promises and proving that God had power over life and death.

Jesus said to her [Mary], "I [Christ] am the resurrection and the life. He who believes in me will live, even though he dies; and whoever lives and believes in me will never die." (John 11:25-26)

This passage has four major gospel truths. In Scripture, the word, *life,* is synonymous with *salvation. First,* Christ is the Source of the resurrection; *second,* He is the Source of salvation, which is spiritual life; *third,* everyone who trusts in Christ will be saved; *fourth,* everyone who has faith in Christ will have eternal life: they will never *die.* In this case, Jesus is not talking about physical death; here the word *die* relates to spiritual death, which is separation from God.

Jesus is the Christ, the promised and long-awaited Messiah. He has come to bring life or salvation; He has come to bring eternal life, so that we shall never *die.*

When we consider the Cross of Christ, we must recognize all the reasons the Christ came into the world. His earthly ministry is too rich a subject without fully seeing all the reasons for His Advent.

This subject deserves our full attention. There are at least twenty reasons that Christ came into the world. However, *to die for the sins of the world* must always be treated as of *first importance.*

Also, on the Cross of Christ, there was the divine exchange that was/is an amazing transformation. On the cross, Christ was the Righteousness of God: standing before the cross, we are sinners in need of redemption. On the cross, Christ *took* on our sins, and He *gave* us His righteousness. We *confess and repent* of our sins: we *receive* His righteousness. Can anyone understand that? Why would Christ exchange His righteousness for our sins? It is all because of love.

Therefore, the Cross of Christ takes on an unbelievable significance for salvation and for eternity.

The gospel accounts (Matt 10:38; Mark 10:21; Luke 14:27) remind us that Jesus spoke of the cross before His death as an example of the commitment required of those who could be His disciples. But the major significance of the cross after Jesus' death and resurrection is its use as a symbol of Jesus' willingness to suffer for our sins (Phil 2:8; Heb 12:2) so that we might be reconciled (2 Cor 5:19; Col 1:20) to God and know His peace (Eph 2:16).

Therefore, the Cross of Christ symbolizes the glory of the Christian gospel (1 Cor 1:17); the fact that through this cruel and inhumane death (1 Cor 1:23; Gal 5:11), the debt of sin against us was *nailed to the cross* (Col 2:14), and we, having *been crucified with Christ* (Gal 2:20), have been freed from sin and death and made alive to God (Rom 6:6-11).

The cross, then, is the symbol of Jesus' love, God's power to save, and the thankful believer's unreserved commitment to Christian discipleship. To those who know the salvation which Christ gained for us through His death, it is a *wondrous cross* indeed.

Christ is not only the Savior of the world, but He is the Word of God who revealed the glory of God.

Such is the divine nature of Christ, who is the Living Word, who is the image of the invisible God, who is the One for whom all things are made, who is the Head of the Body, the church, and who has reconciled to Himself all things, making peace by His blood, shed on the Cross.

In summary, Christ has unquestioned authority, given to Him from the Father. It is by His authority that the gospel message has been preached and its message fulfilled in the lives of all people who love God and who receive and believe in the name of Jesus Christ (John 1:12).

The Cross of Christ is the witness to the world of the sovereignty of God and the love of God.

I close with a quote from my friend, Dr. John Stott.

He knew Himself to be Lord of all, but He became the servant of all.

He came to judge the world, but He washed His disciples' feet.

He renounced the joys of heaven for the sorrows of earth.

He was born of a lowly Hebrew mother in a dirty stable in the insignificant village of Bethlehem.

He became a refugee baby in Egypt; reared in the obscure village of Nazareth; toiled at a carpenter's bench; became an itinerant preacher, with few possessions, small comfort, and no home.

He made friends with simple fisherman, publicans; He touched lepers and allowed harlots to touch Him.

He gave Himself away to a ministry of healing, helping, teaching, and preaching.

He was misunderstood, misinterpreted, and became the victim of men's prejudices.

He was despised and rejected by His own people and deserted, in His hour of need, by His own friends.

He gave His back to be flogged, His face to be spat upon, His head to be crowned with thorns, His hands and His feet to be nailed to a common Roman cross---

And as the cruel spikes were driven home, He kept praying—"Father, forgive them, for they know not what they do."

This utter disregard of self in the service of God and man is called love.

This is love which is in deed and in truth.

This is love which leads to life and self-sacrifice.

There is no love without self-sacrifice; there is no church without evangelism.

His character is totally consistent with His claim.

He is truly the Son of God; He is truly the Savior of the world; He is truly King of kings and Lord of lords.

We now turn to our fourth doctrine, The Power of the Holy Spirit.

Chapter 5

The Power of the Holy Spirit

Do not cast me from your presence, or take your Holy Spirit from me. Restore to me the joy of your salvation and grant me a willing spirit, to sustain me. (Ps 51:11-12)

And afterward, I will pour out my Spirit on all people....And everyone who calls on the name of the LORD will be saved; (Joel 2:28, 32)

I [John the Baptist] baptize you with water for repentance. But after me will come one who is more powerful than I, whose sandals I am not fit to carry. He [Christ] will baptize you with the Holy Spirit and with fire. (Matt 3:11)

But you [disciples of Christ] will receive power when the Holy Spirit comes on you; and you will be my witnesses in Jerusalem, and in all Judea and Samaria, and to the ends of the earth. (Acts 1:8)

The Holy Spirit, as the third person of the Trinity, exercises the power of the Father and the Son in creation, redemption, and reconciliation. The Holy Spirit produces transformation in the lives of Christians and equips all Christians to know the truth and to walk in His power. We are to be led by the Spirit; we are to be transformed by the Spirit; we are to become a new creation by the power of the Spirit.

Who is this Spirit of God? When was He present in Creation? When does He come into the lives of repentant believers? What is His role in the world? These we shall discuss.

Consider the passages at the beginning of this chapter.

Psalm 51 presents this message: first, the importance of the Holy Spirit in the lives of God's people; second, the Holy Spirit is the Source of the joy of God's salvation; third, the Holy Spirit is the Source of God's spirit within me; fourth, the Holy Spirit encourages and sustains the people of God.

Joel 2:28-32 is the promise from God that He will pour out His Spirit on all flesh. Such will equip the people of God with power: further, anyone who calls on the name of the Lord will be saved.

The passage in Matthew 3:11 confirms that Jesus Christ is our Baptizer, and that we received the Holy Spirit as the gift of God at our baptism.

Acts 1:8 is the confirmation that, through the power of the Holy Spirit, we will be equipped to serve as Christ's witnesses to the world.

The Spirit of God was present at Creation (Gen 1:2); the Spirit was promised to all flesh by God (Joel 2:28); the Spirit is given at baptism by Christ; the Spirit of God is given to all who would witness to the Cross of Christ; the Spirit of God will lead all believers into becoming a new creation (Gal 6:15).

The primary functions of the Holy Spirit are to give power to Christians (Acts 1:8), to lead Christians into all truth (John 16:13), and to empower Christians to become a new creation (Gal 6:15), so that they can live a life pleasing to God and so that they can witness to the gospel and advance the kingdom of God.

In addition, the Holy Spirit will convict the world of sin and bring glory to Jesus Christ (John 16:8, 14).

The Holy Spirit was promised by God in Joel 2:28ff; that promise is fulfilled every time a believer is baptized. The completeness of baptism is fully demonstrated by receiving the Spirit of God.

Consider the baptism of Christ and our baptism.

First, the sinless Son of God did not need to be baptized for the remission of sins: He who knew no sin became sin for us. At His baptism, Christ became the example for baptism: what He experienced is what we shall experience. Therefore, recall the event at His baptism. *When all the people were being baptized, Jesus was baptized too. And as he was praying, heaven was opened and the Holy Spirit descended on him in bodily form like a dove. And a voice came from heaven: "You are my Son, whom I love; with you I am well pleased." (Luke 3:21-22)*

The Holy Spirit descended on Jesus Christ at His baptism; in like manner, the Holy Spirit will *descend* on us at our baptism. This truth, that the Spirit is the gift of God at baptism, is confirmed by several examples in the Book of Acts. Consider the following:

At the close of Peter's witness at the first Christian Pentecost in Acts 2, the people turned to Peter. *When the people heard this, they were cut to the heart and said to Peter and the other apostles, "Brothers, what shall we do?" Peter replied, "Repent and be baptized, every one of you, in the name of Jesus Christ for the forgiveness of your sins. And you will receive the gift of the Holy Spirit. The promise is for you and your children and for all who are far off — for all whom the Lord our God will call." (Acts 2:37-39)*

The second example concerned certain disciples in Ephesus, who had received John's baptism but had not heard of the Holy Spirit. Consider the following account.

While Apollos was at Corinth, Paul took the road through the interior and arrived at Ephesus. There he found some disciples and asked them, "Did you receive the Holy Spirit when you believed?" They answered, "No, we have not even heard that there is a Holy Spirit." So Paul asked, "Then what baptism did you receive?" "John's baptism," they replied. Paul said, "John's baptism was a baptism of repentance. He told the people to believe in the one coming after him, that is, in Jesus." On hearing this, they were baptized into the name of the Lord Jesus. When Paul placed his hands on them, the Holy Spirit came on them, and they spoke in tongues and prophesied. (Acts 19:1-6)

What is this baptism at which time we receive the Holy Spirit?

There are two ways in which baptism is viewed and they are complementary. The first is as death and resurrection; the second is as a change of allegiance.

Consider the first: death and resurrection. We die to the old; we rise to the new. We go under the water and we die to the old self. We rise out of the water, resurrection, and are now alive in Christ. We die and we rise again.

Consider the second: a change of allegiance. We enter the water, professing allegiance to one *ruler;* we rise out of the water, professing a new allegiance to Christ. We experience a total change of allegiance; we turn from the things of this world; we turn to the things of God. We set our sight on the spiritual things for which we were created.

We are now His forever, sealed with and by the Holy Spirit (Eph 4:30).

And do not grieve the Holy Spirit of God, with whom you were sealed for the day of redemption. (Eph 4:30)

The Spirit which we have received has four primary functions. The first is to convict the world of sin (John 16:8); the second is to lead Christians into all truth (John 16:13); the third is to bring glory to Christ (John 16:14); the fourth is to be the *Author* of all Scripture (2 Peter 1:20-21).

When he comes, he will convict the world of guilt in regard to sin and righteousness and judgment (John 16:8)....But when he, the Spirit of truth, comes, he will guide you into all truth (John 16:13)....He will bring glory to me (Christ) by taking from what is mine and making it known to you (John 16:14).

At the coming of the Holy Spirit, the triune God of Father, Son, and Holy Spirit are unified in ministering to believers (John 14:16, 26).

The Spirit leads us in the following ways:

First, we are people who live by faith in Christ. *"I have been crucified with Christ and I no longer live, but Christ lives in me. The life I live in the body, I live by faith in the Son of God, who loved me and gave himself for me." (Gal 2:20-21)*

Second, we look to the Spirit so that Christ would be formed in us. *"My dear children, for whom I am again in the pains of childbirth until Christ is formed in you." (Gal 4:19)*

Third, we are to live by the Spirit. *"Since we live by the Spirit, let us keep in step with the Spirit." (Gal 5:25)*

Fourth, by the work of the Spirit within us, we will become a new creation. *"Neither circumcision nor uncircumcision means anything; what counts is a new creation." (Gal 6:15)* By becoming a new creation, we are no longer to sin: instead, we are alive in Christ.

Fifth, it is by the Spirit that we receive power to become a *witness* for Jesus Christ. *"But you will receive power when the Holy Spirit comes on you; and you will be my witnesses in Jerusalem, and in all Judea and Samaria, and to the ends of the earth." (Acts 1:8)*

Sixth, it is by the Spirit that we are *born again* or born spiritually, so that we can see and enter the Kingdom of God *(John 3:1-8)*. The Spirit brings a person to a new spiritual birth: *"That which is born of the flesh is flesh, and that which is born of the Spirit is spirit." (John 3:6);*

Seventh, It is the Spirit who gives life *(John 6:63)*. In Scripture, *life* is synonymous with *salvation*. So the passage reads: *"It is the Spirit who gives salvation."*

Eighth, we see the Spirit as the *Author* of Scripture *(2 Peter 1:20-21)*.

Ninth, the Spirit of God is the Breath of God which signifies God's power and is in striking contrast to heathen gods, which have neither power nor life. The word, *breath,* may be used figuratively, as when Jesus *breathed* the Holy Spirit upon His disciples (John 20:22).

Further, the breath of God is symbolic of the manner which defines the origin of Scripture.

All Scripture is God-breathed and is useful for teaching, rebuking, correcting and training in righteousness, so that the man of God may be thoroughly equipped for every good work. (2 Tim 3:16-4:1)

So the Spirit of God is the gift from God to lead believers into all righteousness so that we would have the truth of God and the power of the Spirit to be witnesses to the Son of God—and proclaim that witness throughout the world.

Above all, evangelism is the evidence of the power of the Spirit to witness to the Son of God.

The Spirit is the divine means by which He witnesses to both the believer and the lost. He encourages the witness to know when to speak, what to say, and how to express it. In addition, the Spirit convicts the lost of the need for redemption and reconciliation.

The Spirit speaks to both.

PART 2
The Gospel of Christ

Chapter 6

The Purpose of the Gospel

For God so loved the world that he gave his one and only Son, that whoever believes in him shall not perish but have eternal life. For God did not send his Son into the world to condemn the world, but to save the world through him. (John 3:16-17)

Jesus said to him, "Today salvation has come to this house, because this man, too, is a son of Abraham. For the Son of Man came to seek and to save what was lost." (Luke 19:9-10)

Jesus answered, "You [Pilate] are right in saying I am a king. In fact, for this reason I was born, and for this I came into the world, to testify to the truth. Everyone on the side of truth listens to me." (John 18:37)

The purpose of the gospel of Christ is abundantly clear. It is the redemption and reconciliation of sinful man with the holy God. Consider the following progression of events.

God created, and He described the results as *good (1:3, 9, 12, 18, 22, 25, 27)*. When God completed His creation, He said that it was *very good.*

However, sin in the form of Satan, the serpent, convinced Eve that she could be like God and know good and evil.

For God knows that when you eat of it your eyes will be opened, and you will be like God, knowing good and evil. (Gen 3:5)

So Adam and Eve did know good and evil: this was the original sin that permeated God's creation.

But the result of sin is spiritual death, which is separation from God. However, Christ came that we would be redeemed and reconciled to God and have the gift of eternal life.

Hear the word of the Lord.

For the wages of sin is death, but the gift of God is eternal life in Christ Jesus our Lord. (Rom 6:23)

Everyone who sins breaks the law; in fact, sin is lawlessness. But you know that he [Christ] appeared so that he might take away our sins. And in him is no sin. (1 John 3:4-6)

Sin is lawlessness; the product of sin is evil and wickedness. Sin stands opposed to God and to His gospel; not only that, the godless will persecute those who proclaim the gospel.

The result of sin is death; knowing Christ is eternal life.

Sin opposes God and His work of righteousness in the world (Rom 7:8-19).

Sin is disobedience and defiance of the will of God.

Sin is rampant and captures the hearts and souls of the unfaithful.

Hear the word of the Lord. The Bible contains 454 passages, documenting the evil that was and is present in the hearts of men. Consider just a few references.

The LORD saw how great man's wickedness on the earth had become, and that every inclination of the thoughts of his heart was only evil all the time. (Gen 6:5)

The Israelites did evil in the eyes of the LORD; they forgot the LORD their God and served the Baals and the Asherahs. The anger of the LORD burned against Israel. (Judges 3:7-8)

You are not a God who takes pleasure in evil; with you the wicked cannot dwell. (Psa 5:4)

From their callous hearts comes iniquity; the evil conceits of their minds know no limits. (Psa 73:7)

I [God] will punish the world for its evil, the wicked for their sins. (Isa 13:11)

The people of Judah have done evil in my eyes, declares the LORD. They have set up their detestable idols in the house that bears my Name and have defiled it. (Jer 7:30)

For from within, out of men's hearts, come evil thoughts, sexual immorality, theft, murder, adultery, greed, malice, deceit, lewdness, envy, slander, arrogance and folly. All these evils come from inside and make a man "unclean." (Mark 7:21-23)

Everyone who does evil hates the light, and will not come into the light for fear that his deeds will be exposed. (John 3:20)

The wrath of God is being revealed from heaven against all the godlessness and wickedness of men who suppress the truth by their wickedness, since what may be known about God is plain to them, because God has made it plain to them. (Rom 1:18-19)

The coming of the lawless one [Satan] will be in accordance with the work of Satan displayed in all kinds of counterfeit miracles, signs and wonders, and in every sort of evil that deceives those who are perishing. They perish because they refused to love the truth and so be saved. (2 Thess 2:9-10)

Dear friend, do not imitate what is evil but what is good. Anyone who does what is good is from God. Anyone who does what is evil has not seen God. (3 John 11)

The evil and wickedness described in the Bible is not just describing the people in that age; no, those characteristics apply to everyone who has ever lived. The Bible speaks to us today; the evil then is the evil now.

The Scriptures emphasize that mankind is essentially evil; the apostle Paul summarized this condition in Romans 1:29-32 and Galatians 5:19-21. Consider the litany of evil.

They have become filled with every kind of wickedness, evil, greed and depravity. They are full of envy, murder, strife, deceit and malice. They are gossips, slanderers, God-haters, insolent, arrogant and boastful; they invent ways of doing evil; they disobey their parents; they are senseless, faithless, heartless, ruthless. Although they know God's righteous decree that those who do such things deserve death, they not only continue to do these very things but also approve of those who practice them. (Rom 1:29-32)

The acts of the sinful nature are obvious: sexual immorality, impurity and debauchery; idolatry and witchcraft; hatred, discord, jealousy, fits of rage, selfish ambition, dissensions, factions and envy; drunkenness, orgies, and the like. I warn you, as I did before, that those who live like this will not inherit the kingdom of God. (Gal 5:19-21)

This litany lists those who are *God-haters*. They just don't resist God or ignore God; they hate God. And this hatred is expressed in persecution of those who follow God.

God will fully and completely deal with evil; He will not ignore forever the evil hearts of men.

Psalm 1 concludes with this passage: *For the LORD watches over the way of the righteous, but the way of the wicked will perish.*

Evil hearts lead to evil acts. Consider a few of the sinful events described in Scripture.

First, the sinful events described in Scripture:

Creation had hardly been completed before evil and wickedness entered. It began in the Garden of Eden and progressively led to wickedness of unparalleled proportions.

Consider Adam and Eve. They were created and instructed by God but they accepted the lies of the devil. Adam and Eve listened to false promises (that they would be like God), and they became the victims of their own pride, rebellion, and disobedience.

Consider the state of mankind prior to the Flood.

The LORD saw how great man's wickedness on the earth had become, and that every inclination of the thoughts of his heart was only evil all the time. The LORD was grieved that he had made man on the earth, and his heart was filled with pain. So the LORD said, "I will wipe mankind, whom I have created, from the face of the earth — men and animals, and creatures that move along the ground, and birds of the air — for I am grieved that I have made them. (Gen 6:5-7)

The evil in the world brought grief to the heart of God: it was true then; it is true today.

In Genesis chapters 1 and 2, the Lord saw that everything that He had made was good; now the Lord *grieved...and his heart was filled with pain.* The condition of mankind, from the beginning of Creation, has not improved with the passing ages.

Consider the Exodus. The Israelites had no sooner left Egypt than they built a golden calf to worship. Moses warned the Israelites: *If you ever forget the LORD your God and follow other gods and worship and bow down to them, I testify against you today that you will surely be destroyed. Like the nations the LORD destroyed before you, so you will be destroyed for not obeying the LORD your God. (Deut 8:19-20)*

During the Exodus, Moses warned the Israelites: *Remember this and never forget how you provoked the LORD your God to anger in the desert. .... you have been rebellious against the LORD. At Horeb you aroused the LORD's wrath so that he was angry enough to destroy you..... Then the LORD told me, "Go down from here at once, because your people whom you brought out of Egypt have become corrupt. They have turned away quickly from what I [God] commanded them and have made a cast idol for themselves." (Deut 9:7-12)*

During the Exodus, the Israelites saw the Promised Land, but they listened to the ten spies rather than to God, who spoke through Joshua and Caleb. As a result, all who lacked faith in God spent their remaining years in the wilderness, and only a new and faithful generation entered the Promised Land. They murmured and grumbled against God (Exo 17:3-7)

What was true then will be true now. Only the faithful will enter the Promised Land: the New Heaven and the New Earth and the New Jerusalem. The Promised Land then, and the Promised Land now, is reserved only for those who love and trust and obey and serve God.

God has constantly warned His people of the consequences of unfaithfulness. However, rarely have the warnings been obeyed.

Consider the warning of Joshua to the Israelites: *throw away the gods your forefathers worshiped.*

Now fear the LORD and serve him with all faithfulness. Throw away the gods your forefathers worshiped beyond the River and in Egypt, and serve the LORD....then choose for yourselves this day whom you will serve, whether the gods your forefathers served beyond the River, or the gods of the Amorites, in whose land you are living. But as for me and my household, we will serve the LORD. (Josh 24:14-15)

Consider the golden age of the Israelites under David. Evil arose, wickedness persisted, and the United Kingdom was divided into the northern Kingdom of Israel and the southern Kingdom of Judah. Evil dominated both kingdoms. Rebellion and disobedience to God continued. Therefore the northern Kingdom of Israel fell to the Assyrians in 722 BC, and the southern Kingdom of Judah fell to the Babylonians in 586 BC. Sin and lawlessness had so permeated the two kingdoms that they fell, never to arise again.

The Israelites were "*stiff-necked*" (Exo 32:9 to Jer 19:15) a total of 18 times in Scripture; "*rebellious*" (Num 17:10 to Zeph 3:1) a total of 41 times in Scripture, and "*disobedient*" (Neh 9:26).

"I have seen these people," the LORD said to Moses, "and they are a stiff-necked people. Now leave me alone so that my [God's] anger may burn against them and that I may destroy them. Then I will make you into a great nation." (Ex 32:9-10)

But these people have stubborn and rebellious hearts; they have turned aside and gone away. They do not say to themselves, 'Let us fear the LORD our God,' (Jer 5:23-24)

But they were disobedient and rebelled against you; they put your law behind their backs. They killed your prophets, who had admonished them in order to turn them back to you; they committed awful blasphemies. (Neh 9:26)

However, the characteristics (stiff-necked, rebellious, and disobedient) do not apply to the Israelites alone. Again, they apply to the world today.

In spite of the evil in the hearts of man, God sought our redemption and reconciliation.

That could only be accomplished through the Cross of Christ.

Consider Jesus Christ, the Son of God, who came into the world to redeem the world from sin and to reconcile repentant sinners to God. The Bible speaks of His rejection by His own people. The chief priest and the elders sought to kill Him (Matt 26:4); they finally did. They crucified Him.

He [Christ] was in the world, and though the world was made through him, the world did not recognize him. He came to that which was his own, but his own did not receive him. Yet to all who received him, to those who believed in his name, he gave the right to become children of God— children born not of natural descent, nor of human decision or a husband's will, but born of God. (John 1:10-13)

Christ came to His own, but His own received Him not. They did not recognize nor acknowledge the One through whom the world had been made and the One through whom the world would be made new (Rev 22:1-4).

The Jews savagely and brutally rejected the Messiah, sent by God.

And, since that time, many have rejected the Son of God. However, the opposite is equally true; many have joyfully received the King of kings and Lord of lords as their Savior and Lord. The righteous love Him, honor Him, obey Him, serve Him, and witness to Him.

The gospel contains a series of great truths, which we have just discussed. However, it has a unique purpose which Paul captures in the Epistle to the Galatians. The purpose is associated with the fact that Christ came to rescue us from this evil age and, if we accept the gospel, we will become a new creation (2 Cor 5:17; Gal 6:15) and we will be reconciled to God and we will have everlasting life.

In the Epistle to the Galatians, Paul identifies four transformations that will occur as we accept the gospel. First, the gospel will lead us to be a *person of faith (3:9)*; second, *Christ would be formed in us (4:19)*; third, *we would live by the Spirit (5:16)*; fourth, *we would be a new creation (6:15)*.

It is this transformation, Paul said, that enables us to know the gospel, to accept the gospel, to live according to the gospel, and to proclaim the gospel to those who are presently in darkness.

A companion purpose is that we would become ministers of reconciliation to take the gospel to those who have not heard it.

Therefore, if anyone is in Christ, he is a new creation; the old has gone, the new has come! All this is from God, who reconciled us to himself through Christ and gave us the ministry of reconciliation: that God was reconciling the world to himself in Christ, not counting men's sins against them. And he has committed to us the message of reconciliation. We are therefore Christ's ambassadors, as though God were making his appeal through us. We implore you on Christ's behalf: Be reconciled to God. God made him who had no sin to be sin for us, so that in him we might become the righteousness of God. (2 Cor 5:17-21)

How beautiful on the mountains are the feet of those who bring good news, who proclaim peace, who bring good tidings, who proclaim salvation, who say to Zion, 'Your God reigns!' (Isa 52:7)

As we fulfill our responsibility to evangelize, God emphasizes that He would be found by a people who did not seek Him. This will culminate in what is called the great *"mystery of the gospel" (Romans 11:25-30)*. The Bible emphasizes that God will gather all the nations to Him and He will judge the nations with justice and equity.

Because the gospel is universal and eternal, the Scriptures contain many passages, relating to God seeking and calling to all nations.

And Isaiah boldly says, "I [God] was found by those who did not seek me; I revealed myself to those who did not ask for me." But concerning Israel he says, "All day long I have held out my hands to a disobedient and obstinate people." (Rom 10:20)

Now to him who is able to establish you by my gospel and the proclamation of Jesus Christ, according to the revelation of the mystery hidden for long ages past, but now revealed and made known through the prophetic writings by the command of the eternal God, so that all nations might believe and obey him— to the only wise God be glory forever through Jesus Christ! Amen. (Rom 16:25-27)

And he made known to us the mystery of his will according to his good pleasure, which he purposed in Christ, to be put into effect when the times will have reached their fulfillment — to bring all things in heaven and on earth together under one head, even Christ. (Eph 1:9-10)

In reading this, then, you will be able to understand my insight into the mystery of Christ, which was not made known to men in other generations as it has now been revealed by the Spirit to God's holy apostles and prophets. This mystery is that through the gospel the Gentiles are heirs together with Israel, members together of one body, and sharers together in the promise in Christ Jesus. (Eph 3:4-6)

Beyond all question, the mystery of godliness is great: He [Christ] appeared in a body, was vindicated by the Spirit, was seen by angels, was preached among the nations, was believed on in the world, was taken up in glory. (1 Tim 3:15-16)

So what is the purpose of the gospel?

It is to rescue us from this present evil age; it is *to deliver* us from the power of Satan; it is *to protect* us from temptations; it is *to provide* us with divine gifts; it is *to equip* us to love and serve the holy God; it is *to redeem* and *reconcile* sinful man to the holy God.

Why does God seek this? He does this because He is the God of love. That is His nature, and He cannot go against His nature.

How will God achieve this? By sending His only begotten Son, to die on the cross for the sins of the world and to give us His righteousness.

Chapter 7

The gospel is the power of God for salvation of everyone who believes (Rom 1:16)

For God so loved the world that he gave his one and only Son, that whoever believes in him shall not perish but have eternal life. (John 3:16)

Believe in the Lord Jesus, and you will be saved — you and your household (Acts 16:31)

I am not ashamed of the gospel, because it is the power of God for the salvation of everyone who believes: first for the Jew, then for the Gentile. For in the gospel a righteousness from God is revealed, a righteousness that is by faith from first to last, just as it is written: "The righteous will live by faith." (Rom 1:16-17)

That if you confess with your mouth, "Jesus is Lord," and believe in your heart that God raised him from the dead, you will be saved. (Rom 10:9)

For it is by grace you have been saved, through faith — and this not from yourselves, it is the gift of God. (Eph 2:8)

And this gospel of the kingdom will be preached in the whole world as a testimony to all nations, and then the end will come. (Matt 24:14)

The beginning of the gospel about Jesus Christ, the Son of God....
(Mark 1:1)

The Scripture foresaw that God would justify the Gentiles by faith, and announced the gospel in advance to Abraham: "All nations will be blessed through you." So those who have faith are blessed along with Abraham, the man of faith. Understand, then, that those who believe are children of Abraham. (Gal 3:6-9)

And you also were included in Christ when you heard the word of truth, the gospel of your salvation. Having believed, you were marked in him with a seal, the promised Holy Spirit, who is a deposit guaranteeing our inheritance until the redemption of those who are God's possession — to the praise of his glory. (Eph 1:13-14)

Then I saw another angel flying in midair, and he had the eternal gospel to proclaim to those who live on the earth — to every nation, tribe, language and people. (Rev 14:6)

We now come to the discussion of the gospel of Christ, the most glorious message of hope and confidence that the world has ever heard. There is no message since the beginning of time that matches these thoughts of grace and mercy and faith and salvation.

First, consider the gospel messages in the biblical passages at the beginning of this chapter.

In John 3:16, we find that the gift of God, His Son, is given because God loves His creation. His great love is reflected in His great gift.

In Acts 16:31, we find the truth that belief in Christ is the foundation of salvation.

Romans 1:16-17 defined the gospel of Christ as well as the message of the gospel.

In Romans 10:9, we find the truth that confession of faith in Christ and belief in His resurrection are the keys to salvation.

In Ephesians 2:8, we find the trilogy of grace, faith, and salvation. God's grace and our response in faith is the basis of salvation.

In Matt 24:14, Jesus Christ stated that the gospel will be preached universally before the end of this age.

Mark 1:1 affirms that the centerpiece of the gospel is Jesus Christ, the Son of God.

Galatians 3:6-9 confirms that the gospel was first announced through Abraham, that all nations would be blessed, justified, through the offspring of Abraham, who was Jesus Christ.

Revelation 14:6 identifies the gospel of Christ as an eternal gospel, which began through Abraham but which is everlasting in purpose. The gospel of Christ is available to all people today and throughout the ages.

The richness of these passages comes alive in the gospel of Christ. God has spoken to the world through this good news, which shall be for all people, and He has extended His Arm to reach all with His love. It is His perfect patience that no one should perish but that all should come to salvation through faith in His Son, Jesus Christ (2 Pet 3:9).

The world has never fully accepted this gospel message; regardless of the reaction, Christians are called to be Christ's ambassadors for redemption and reconciliation.

So what is this gospel, this message that we proclaim to the world? What is this *good news?* Why should we accept it? Why should we proclaim it?

The gospel of Christ is the good news from God that reflects His love for His creation and was given *to rescue* us from this present evil age. It was given *to deliver* us from the power of evil; it was given *to protect* us from temptation; it was given *to provide* us with the Holy Spirit; it was given *to equip* us for every good work; it was given *to empower* us to be faithful children of the holy and sovereign God.

The message of the gospel of Christ: God is prepared to love us, to deliver us, to forgive us, to redeem us, to reconcile us, to protect us, to provide for us, to equip us, and to empower us.

The word, gospel, means *the story concerning God.* It is the proclamation of the forgiveness of sins and reconciliation with God. Forgiveness and reconciliation are two interconnected events. Through the Cross of Christ, we become the righteousness of God. Through the gift of the Holy Spirit, we become the children of God.

The word, gospel, is derived from the Anglo-Saxon word, *godspel,* which means *a message from God or the story concerning God.* However, consider the word, *godspel.* If the *d* is removed, the word becomes *gospel.* Gospel truly means a message sent from God. However, in addition, the word, gospel, is rightly taken to mean *good news* which brings great joy. When these two thoughts are combined, the conclusion is: *the gospel is a message from God which brings good news and great joy to the hearer.*

In the New Testament the Greek word, *euaggelion,* means *good news.* It proclaims good news of deliverance from sin and entrance into the Kingdom of God; it proclaims redemption and reconciliation with God. Once alienated from God; now restored to God.

The gospel confirms the promises and prophecies of God; it also confirms our responsibility to proclaim the gospel and to advance the Kingdom.

The gospel offers salvation through the grace of God to everyone who believes.

For it is by grace you have been saved, through faith — and this not from yourselves, it is the [free] gift of God— not by works, so that no one can boast. For we are God's workmanship, created in Christ Jesus to do good works, which God prepared in advance for us to do. (Eph 2:8-10)

The gospel reveals God's love and glory; the gospel defines eternity.

The message of the gospel defines the basis of salvation, which calls for our faith as our response to the grace of God.

Grace and faith lead to salvation.

The gospel is a message of Old Testament promises and New Testament fulfillments.

The gospel is the message of God's love, revealed throughout history and centered in His Son. The gospel is the truth about divine love. The Cross of Christ and the resurrection of Christ are the central themes of the gospel. Understand Christ's death and His resurrection, and we will understand the gospel.

The word, *gospel*, is recorded 96 times in the Bible, but only in the New Testament. However, the word also stands for *good news*, which is recorded 36 times in both the Old and New Testament and is equivalent to the word, *gospel*. Consider some of the relevant passages which deal with the equivalence of *good news* with the word, *gospel*.

How beautiful on the mountains are the feet of those who bring good news, who proclaim peace, who bring good tidings, who proclaim salvation, who say to Zion, "Your God reigns!" (Isa 52:7)

Jesus went throughout Galilee, teaching in their synagogues, preaching the good news of the kingdom, and healing every disease and sickness among the people. (Matt 4:23)

He [Jesus] said to them, "Go into all the world and preach the good news to all creation. Whoever believes and is baptized will be saved, but whoever does not believe will be condemned." (Mark 16:15-16)

But he [Jesus] said, "I must preach the good news of the kingdom of God to the other towns also, because that is why I was sent." (Luke 4:43)

So the terms, *gospel* and *good news*, are interchangeable and express the same truth.

Jesus Christ came to preach the gospel: His ministry is now our ministry.

The word, gospel, originally stood for the recorded life and ministry of Jesus Christ (Mark 1:1) and included the events in His life, as well as His teachings. Rarely did these writings of Matthew, Mark, Luke, and John discuss the theology behind the events in Christ's life, so these books were initially considered historical accounts of the life of Jesus. In fact, Luke wrote a two-volume account, which he entitled the *History of Christianity.* Volume 1 documented the earthly life of Christ, while volume 2 was the life of the Church, under the power of the Holy Spirit. Volume 1 became the Gospel according to Luke, while Volume 2 became the Acts of the Apostles.

However, the word, *gospel*, came to be used for certain writings in which the *good news* or the story of Jesus Christ was told. These documents, mostly written in the first century AD, became known as *gospel* much later, perhaps in the second and third century AD.

The New Testament then had a record of the four versions of the one gospel, which we now call the Gospel according to Matthew, Mark, Luke, and John. Each of these four versions presents Jesus Christ in uniquely different manners. For example, Matthew presents Jesus Christ as King: *Behold, thy King (Zech 9:9)*; Mark presents Him as the Servant: *Behold, thy Servant (Isa 42:1)*; Luke, as the Man: *Behold, the Man (Zech 6:12)*; and John, as God: *Behold, your God (Isa 40:1)*.

Now, with time, the term, *gospel,* took on a different tone, by defining the theology relative to the birth, earthly life, ministry, death, resurrection, and ascension of Jesus Christ.

Finally, the word, *gospel,* described primarily the message which Christianity proclaims. *Good news* is its significance. It is a message from God which, when accepted, results in a gift from God. It is the proclamation of the forgiveness of sins and sonship with God restored through Christ. It now meant forgiveness of sins, redemption and reconciliation with God. The *gospel* now becomes a message of salvation, and the means through which the Holy Spirit works (Rom 1:16).

The centerpiece of the gospel is the Cross of Christ. It is the event to which the Old Testament points; it is the event from which everything in the New Testament follows.

The resurrection is the foundation of the conviction that Jesus is the Christ, the Son of the living God.

The gospel, then, is the message of God, the teaching of Christianity, the redemption in and by Jesus Christ, the only begotten Son of God, offered to all mankind. And as the gospel is bound up in the life of Christ, It is His biography, the record of His works, and the proclamation of what He has to offer.

It is the joyful good news of salvation in and through Jesus Christ.

Christ began His earthly ministry by calling people to repentance (Matt 4:17). Repentance is the basis of forgiveness; without repentance, forgiveness will never occur. Later, Christ followed this warning by proclaiming His gospel of salvation when He read the following from the prophet Isaiah.

He [Jesus] went to Nazareth, where he had been brought up, and on the Sabbath day he went into the synagogue, as was his custom. And he stood up to read. The scroll of the prophet Isaiah was handed to him. Unrolling it, he found the place where it is written: "The Spirit of the Lord is on me, because he has anointed me to preach good news to the poor. He has sent me to proclaim freedom for the prisoners and recovery of sight for the blind, to release the oppressed, to proclaim the year of the Lord's favor."

Then he rolled up the scroll, gave it back to the attendant and sat down. The eyes of everyone in the synagogue were fastened on him, and he began by saying to them, "Today this scripture is fulfilled in your hearing." (Luke 4:16-21)

This gospel, which is the *good news* that Jesus Christ proclaimed is God's eternal plan of salvation. It is the fulfillment of God's plan of salvation which was announced to Abraham, begun in Israel, completed in Jesus Christ, has been made known to the world by the church, and will be completed with the coming of the New Heaven and the New Earth and the New Jerusalem.

The gospel is the saving work of God in His Son Jesus Christ and a call to faith in Him (Rom 1:16-17). Jesus is more than a messenger of the gospel; He is the gospel. The *good news* of God was present in Christ's life, teaching, atoning death, and resurrection and ascension. Therefore, the gospel is both an historical event and a personal relationship.

To receive the gospel demands faith on our part. However, faith is more than an intellectual agreement to a theoretical truth. Faith is trust placed in a living person, Jesus Christ. When the apostle Paul warned Christians of the dangers of following *another gospel* (2 Cor 11:4), he was reminding them that any gospel different than the one he preached was no gospel at all.

However, the gospel is more than the biography of Jesus Christ, intended to provide information about a historical character. It is the presentation of the life of Jesus to show His saving significance for all people and to call them to faith in Him.

These portraits in the gospel messages present Christ as our Redeemer, our Advocate, and our Savior and our Lord.

However, in presenting the gospel of God, Paul's Epistle to the Romans best captures the theology of the gospel. Saying that, Paul's Epistle to the Galatians is the forerunner to the gospel message which Paul was later to expand and refine in Romans.

As valuable as all the other sources are, this book will emphasize the Epistles to the Romans and the Galatians. Paul's Epistle to the Galatians is his first epistle and was written about 49 AD; while Romans was written in approximately 56-58 AD, about 7 years after his epistle to the Galatians and well before that of any of the other New Testament documents were available.

It is well for us to have some idea of the definition of the gospel, which has been defined by many denominations, by many Christian organizations, and by many Biblical dictionaries. However, this book will use the definition given by the apostle Paul in his Epistle to the Romans.

I am not ashamed of the gospel, because it is the power of God for the salvation of everyone who believes: first for the Jew, then for the Gentile. For in the gospel a righteousness from God is revealed, a righteousness that is by faith from first to last, just as it is written: "The righteous will live by faith." (Rom 1:16-17)

The gospel is the power of God for the salvation of everyone who believes.

The gospel is God's message which He has commissioned His church to proclaim. This proclamation is so that those who had been slaves to sin would become the righteousness of God. God has always desired a relationship of holy love with His created: that relationship can only occur through the redemption and reconciliation of repentant sinners.

That is the purpose of the Cross of Christ.

The earliest form of the gospel message may well have been that which was contained in the epistles of the apostle Paul. Certainly his first epistle to the Galatians defended the gospel, explained the gospel, and outlined a life lived in the power of the gospel. It is also likely that early Christian hymns (Phil 2:6-11) might have been used to present the gospel. Further, the messages contained in Romans 10:9, I Corinthians 12:3, and I Timothy 3:16 may have provided both the basis for gospel presentation as well as the basis for Christian creeds.

Since the word, *gospel*, means good news from God which brings great joy, then one might rightfully argue that there are many biblical passages and many doctrines which meet those criteria.

However, we need to be very careful. There are certain criteria that must be met for such passages to have the recognition as the gospel message.

The criteria that must be preserved must contain at least the following four conditions: first, a historical proclamation of the birth, death, resurrection and ascension of Jesus Christ as determined by Old Testament prophecies and New Testament fulfillment; second, a theological summary of the Person of Jesus Christ as both Savior and Lord; third, an invitation to acknowledge Jesus Christ as our Savior and Lord, to whom every knee shall bow and every tongue confess Him Lord, to the glory of God the Father; fourth, a call to acknowledge sin, to repent, and to receive the forgiveness of sins; for *by grace you have been saved through faith. (Eph 2:8)*

I emphasize that there is one gospel, but I will discuss the gospel from two perspectives.

First, there is the theological gospel, which strengthens the knowledge of the believer. That should not generally be used in witnessing.

Second, there is the summary gospel, which meets the needs of witnessing, and which should contain the basic doctrines for the lost. The lost will generally be in two categories: first, those who face the presence of sin and need forgiveness from sin; second, those who face the absence of the Lord.

So we begin with an explanation of the detailed theology of the gospel.

The Gospel: The Theology
From Abraham to the New Heaven and the
New Earth and the New Jerusalem

We begin the examination of the gospel of Christ, beginning with God's covenant with Abraham in Genesis and ending with the coming of the New Heaven and the New Earth and the New Jerusalem, as revealed in the Book of Revelation.

In its most complete sense, the Scriptures present the *gospel of Christ* through the following sixteen gospel themes:

First: The Covenant with Abraham: all nations (Gen 22:18)

Second: The Promise of the Spirit: all power (Joel 2:28-32)

Third: The Covenant for the Forgiveness of Sin: all forgiveness (Jer 31:31-34)

Fourth, The Promise of the Everlasting Kingdom (Psa 145:13; Dan 7:27)

Fifth, The Promise of the Messiah (Dan 9:24-25)

Sixth, The Incarnation; the Gift of the Son of God: The First Advent (Luke 2:8-14)

Seventh, The Promise of Eternal Life (Dan 12:1-3)

Eight, The New Birth: You must be born again (John 3:5-8)

Ninth, The Cross of Christ (Matt 27:32-50)

Tenth, The Resurrection Of Christ: Eternal life (John 10:26)

Eleventh, The Coming of the Holy Spirit (Acts 2:1-4)

Twelfth, Christ's Second Coming (Acts 1:10)

Thirteenth, The Kingdom of God, the Eternal Kingdom (2 Pet 1:11)

Fourteenth, The General Resurrection (Dan 12:1-3)

Fifthteenth, The Final Judgment: Reward and Punishment (Rev 14:7)

Sixteenth, The New Heaven, The New Earth, the New Jerusalem:
the New Creation (Rev 21:1-4)

Now, we will briefly consider each of these 16 gospel events.

First: The Covenant with Abraham: all nations blessed through Abraham's offspring.

God first announced His gospel to Abraham, because Abraham believed God and Abraham was *the man of faith and obedience.* The gospel promise was that all the nations will be blessed through Abraham and his offspring.

There are two key passages: Galatians 3:6-9 and Genesis 22:17-18.

Consider Abraham: "He believed God, and it was credited to him as righteousness." Understand, then, that those who believe are children of Abraham. The Scripture foresaw that God would justify the Gentiles by faith, and announced the gospel in advance to Abraham: "All nations will be blessed through you." So those who have faith are blessed along with Abraham, the man of faith. (Gal 3:6-9)

Your descendants will take possession of the cities of their enemies, and through your offspring all nations on earth will be blessed, because you have obeyed me. (Gen 22:17-18)

The question is: who is this offspring of Abraham, through whom all the nations will be blessed? We turn to the gospel of Matthew for that answer.

Matthew begins by outlining, in the genealogy of Jesus Christ, the identification of Christ as the *son of Abraham. A record of the genealogy of Jesus Christ the son of David, the son of Abraham: Abraham was the father of Isaac,...16 Matthan the father of Jacob, and Jacob the father of Joseph, the husband of Mary, of whom was born Jesus, who is called Christ.(Matt 1:1-2, 16)*

Jesus Christ, the Son of God, is the *offspring* of Abraham through whom all the nations will be blessed. In addition, the true children of Abraham are the spiritual children of the promise who are regarded as Abraham's offsprings (Romans 9:6-9)

For not all who are descended from Israel are Israel. Nor because they are his descendants are they all Abraham's children. On the contrary, "It is through Isaac that your offspring will be reckoned." In other words, it is not the natural children who are God's children, but it is the children of the promise who are regarded as Abraham's offspring. (Rom 9:6-9)

God's love is the foundation of His gospel; our faith, as with Abraham's faith, ensures our inclusion in God's covenant with Abraham.

The next step in the gospel is the promise of the Holy Spirit.

Second: The Promise of the Spirit: all truth and all power to the redeemed

The second step in the gospel of Christ is the promise of the gift of the Holy Spirit, which God proclaimed through the prophet Joel (841-835 BC): that promised gift was fulfilled in John 14:25-26.

And afterward, I [God] will pour out my Spirit on all people....And everyone who calls on the name of the LORD will be saved; (Joel 2:28-32)

All this I [Christ] have spoken while still with you. But the Counselor, the Holy Spirit, whom the Father will send in my name, will teach you all things and will remind you of everything I have said to you. (John 14:25-26)

As all people will be blessed through Abraham and his offspring, God promised to pour out His Spirit on all flesh. Further, Christ explained the three-fold ministry of the Spirit.

But I [Christ] tell you the truth: It is for your good that I am going away. Unless I go away, the Counselor will not come to you; but if I go, I will send him to you. When he comes, he will convict the world of guilt in regard to sin and righteousness and judgment: ...But when he, the Spirit of truth, comes, he will guide you into all truth....He will bring glory to me [Christ] by taking from what is mine and making it known to you. (John 16:7-15)

So the promise of the Spirit to all flesh sets the stage for the New Covenant.

Third: The New Covenant for the Forgiveness of Sin

This new covenant, proclaimed through the prophet Jeremiah (625-580 BC), had the following five promises: I [God] will make a *new covenant* with my people of faith; *first,* I will be your God and you will be my people; *second,* everyone shall know God; *third,* I shall write my laws on their hearts and not on tablets of stone; *fourth,* I will forgive their iniquities; *fifth,* I will remember their sins no more.

Behold, the days are coming, says the LORD, when I will make a new covenant with the house of Israel and the house of Judah, not like the covenant which I made with their fathers when I took them by the hand to bring them out of the land of Egypt, my covenant which they broke, though I was their husband, says the LORD. But this is the covenant which I will make with the house of Israel after those days, says the LORD: I will put my law within them, and I will write it upon their hearts; and I will be their God, and they shall be my people. And no longer shall each man teach his neighbor and each his brother, saying, 'Know the LORD,' for they shall all know me, from the least of them to the greatest, says the LORD; for I will forgive their iniquity, and I will remember their sin no more. (Jer 31:31-34 RSV)

This new covenant was ratified by the blood shed by Christ on the cross.

Next follows the promise of the everlasting Kingdom of God.

Fourth: The Promise of the Everlasting Kingdom of God

They will tell of the glory of your kingdom and speak of your might, so that all men may know of your mighty acts and the glorious splendor of your kingdom. Your kingdom is an everlasting kingdom, and your dominion endures through all generations. (Ps 145:11-13)

Then the sovereignty, power and greatness of the kingdoms under the whole heaven will be handed over to the saints, the people of the Most High. His kingdom will be an everlasting kingdom, and all rulers will worship and obey him. (Dan 7:27)

The everlasting Kingdom will be present in the New Heaven and the New Earth and the New Jerusalem—and will be ruled by Christ, the Messiah, the Son of God.

With the everlasting kingdom will come the Messiah, the Christ, the everlasting King of the kingdom.

Fifth: The Promise of the Messiah

Seventy 'sevens' are decreed for your people and your holy city to finish transgression, to put an end to sin, to atone for wickedness, to bring in everlasting righteousness, to seal up vision and prophecy and to anoint the most holy. Know and understand this: from the issuing of the decree to restore and rebuild Jerusalem until the Anointed One, the ruler, comes, there will be seven 'sevens,' and sixty-two 'sevens. (Dan 9:24-25)

The Messiah was promised to deliver the redeemed and to live and rule forever. *The [Jewish] crowd spoke up, "We have heard from the Law that the Christ will remain forever." (John 12:34)*

The promised Messiah would ensure that everyone who had faith in Him would have eternal life. That promise will be given to those who receive and believe in the Son.

The next phase in the *gospel of Christ* was the Incarnation of the Son of God. God sent His Son into the world to die for the sins of the world according to the will and plan of God.

Sixth: God Incarnate

The incarnation, the birth of Christ, was the beginning of the fullness of the revelation of the gospel of Christ. His conception was supernatural; His birth was natural. Psalm 2:7 and Isaiah 9:6-7, among other passages, describe the spiritual and physical nature of the birth of Jesus Christ.

I will proclaim the decree of the LORD: He [God] said to me, "You are my Son; today I have become your Father." (Psa 2:7)

For to us a child is born, to us a son is given, and the government will be on his shoulders. And he will be called Wonderful Counselor, Mighty God, Everlasting Father, Prince of Peace. Of the increase of his government and peace there will be no end. He will reign on David's throne and over his kingdom, establishing and upholding it with justice and righteousness from that time on and forever. The zeal of the LORD Almighty will accomplish this. (Isa 9:6-7)

In several New Testament passages (e.g. Matt 1:23 and John 1:14), we find the fulfillment of the prophecy.

The virgin will be with child and will give birth to a son, and they will call him Immanuel-which means, "God with us". (Matt 1:23)

The Word became flesh and made his dwelling among us. We have seen his glory, the glory of the One and Only, who came from the Father, full of grace and truth. (John 1:14)

The angel of the Lord proclaimed the birth of the Lord: *for to you is born this day in the city of David a Savior, who is Christ the Lord.*

The good news is that the Messiah, the Christ, has come into the world. God Himself, fully God and fully man, had been born.

The reason for the birth: that Christ would save the world from sin.

For God so loved the world that he gave his one and only Son, that whoever believes in him shall not perish but have eternal life. For God did not send his Son into the world to condemn the world, but to save the world through him. (John 3:16-17)

The Incarnation expressed the love of God. God not only loved, but He also gave. Loving without giving is incomplete. God's love was expressed in the Light of Christ, which revealed the truth and condemned the darkness.

This Light of the world is both Savior and Lord.

This child, born in Bethlehem, was God Incarnate.

This child, fully divine and fully human, came to die on a cross for the sins of the world.

This child, the Son of God, became like us so that we could become like Him.

The Incarnation of Christ opened the door for the spiritual birth of all who believed in Him (John 1:12), as well as the promise of eternal life.

Seventh: The Promise of Eternal Life

The Scriptures emphasize that the gift of eternal life with God is for the redeemed who have accepted the Christ.

Whoever believes in the Son has eternal life, but whoever rejects the Son will not see life, for God's wrath remains on him. (John 3:36)

I [Christ] tell you the truth, whoever hears my word and believes him who sent me has eternal life and will not be condemned; he has crossed over from death to life." (John 5:24)

My sheep listen to my [Christ] voice; I know them, and they follow me. I give them eternal life, and they shall never perish; no one can snatch them out of my hand. (John 10:27-28)

Now this is eternal life: that they may know you, the only true God, and Jesus Christ, whom you have sent. (John 17:3)

But at that time your people — everyone whose name is found written in the book — will be delivered. Multitudes who sleep in the dust of the earth will awake: some to everlasting life, others to shame and everlasting contempt. (Dan 12:1-3)

Christ's birth opened the door for our spiritual birth, so that we would become children of God (John 1:12).

Eighth: The New Birth: A Child of God

The gospel according to John proclaims this necessity: *you must be born again.* (John 3:7)

This new birth is essential if anyone is to see and enter the Kingdom of God (John 3:3, 5).

The Scriptures emphasize two births (physical and spiritual) and two deaths (physical and spiritual). Christians are born physically and spiritually; Christians can only die physically. Spiritual birth makes us a child of God.

If you are born once (physically), then you will die twice (physically and spiritually). However, if you are born twice (physically and spiritually), then you will only die once (physically).

Jesus said that the new birth is the result of two decisions, closely related. The first decision is to *receive* Jesus Christ as the Messiah, the Son of God. The second decision is to *believe* in His name, which means to trust in Him fully for all things. The two decisions to be made: first, *to believe* in Jesus Christ; second, *to receive* Him as Savior and Lord. When those companion decisions are affirmed, then we become a child of God, born of God and with God as our spiritual Father.

He came to that which was his own, but his own did not receive him. Yet to all who received him, to those who believed in his name, he gave the right to become children of God— children born not of natural descent, nor of human decision or a husband's will, but born of God. (John 1:11-13)

As a result of this spiritual birth, Jesus Christ said that we can now *see* and *enter* the Kingdom of God. The residents of the Kingdom of God are those who have been *born again, born from above, born of the Spirit.*

In reply Jesus declared, "I tell you the truth, no one can see the kingdom of God unless he is born again."...Jesus answered, "I tell you the truth, no one can enter the kingdom of God unless he is born of water and the Spirit. Flesh gives birth to flesh, but the Spirit gives birth to spirit. You should not be surprised at my saying, 'You must be born again.'" (John 3:3-8)

Christ came into the world so that, through Him, we would be born of the Spirit and be able to see and enter the Kingdom of God.

By the spiritual birth, God becomes our Father; we become His children.

All of the eight promises: *The Covenant with Abraham; The Promise of the Spirit; The New Covenant for the Forgiveness of Sin; The Promise of the Everlasting Kingdom; The Promise of the Messiah; The Incarnation; The Promise of Eternal Life; The Second Birth* all lead to the Cross of Christ; their fulfillment of these promises *follow from* the Cross.

The Cross of Christ is the centerpiece of the gospel of Christ.

Ninth, The Cross of Christ

After examining the Cross of Christ, we will see the
gospel passages that flow from that Cross.
Tenth, The Resurrection of Christ: Eternal Life (John 10:26)
Eleventh, The Coming of the Holy Spirit (Acts 2:1-4)
Twelfth, Christ's Second Coming:
Thirteenth, The Kingdom of God, The Eternal Kingdom (2 Pet 1:11)
Fourteenth, The General Resurrection:

Fifthteenth, The Final Judgment: Reward and Punishment
Sixteenth, The New Heaven, The New Earth, the New
Jerusalem: the New Creation (Rev 21:1-3)

Ninth: The Cross of Christ

The Cross of Christ was according to the will and plan of God: it was not the will of man, nor was it any accident of history. This truth is expressed by the Apostle Peter at the first Christian Pentecost.

This man [Jesus Christ] was handed over to you by God's set purpose and foreknowledge; and you, with the help of wicked men, put him to death by nailing him to the cross. But God raised him from the dead, freeing him from the agony of death, because it was impossible for death to keep its hold on him. (Acts 2:23-24)

The Cross of Christ is the ultimate expression of the love of God; this will lead directly to the resurrection, the second coming of Christ, and the New Heaven and the New Earth and the New Jerusalem.

The Cross of Christ is the ultimate good news.

The paradox is that the *death* of the Son of God is the ultimate gospel event.

How can the death of the Son of God be such blessed good news?

Well, it is clearly good news for the repentant sinner. Consider the divine, historic, and supernatural event. Nothing like this has ever happened on earth—and nothing like this will ever happen again.

On the Cross, a divine exchange took place between repentant sinners and the righteous Son of God. Christ was on the cross: we sinners stood before the cross. At an unbelievable moment in divine history, the sinless Son of God took on our sins; we, in exchange, received His righteousness. He who knew no sin became sin for us: we who knew no righteousness became the righteousness of God.

Is that something that we will ever understand? Is that something that we can ever fully appreciate?

We, who were sinners, became righteous. Christ, who knew no sin, became sin for us.

That is why the great darkness covered the earth while the sinless Son of God completed what He had come to complete. That is why Christ said: *it is finished.*

The cross is *good news* in the same way that that the crucifixion is now recognized as the crowning event of *Good Friday.* God did not need to send His Son to the cross, but He did so because God is love and He loves us. Can we ever understand the love of God? Can we ever understand the seriousness of our sins?

Christ's death was that divine act to ratify the new covenant for the forgiveness of sins, proclaimed by God through the prophet Jeremiah.

Jesus spoke often of His coming to die for the sins of the world, e.g.

Jesus said, "This voice was for your benefit, not mine. Now is the time for judgment on this world; now the prince of this world will be driven out. But I, when I am lifted up from the earth, will draw all men to myself." He said this to show the kind of death he was going to die. (John 12:30-33)

He not only spoke of His death, but He also described the manner in which He was to die.

Using the example of Moses in the wilderness (Num 21:4-9), Christ said that He would *be lifted up.*

They [the Israelites] traveled from Mount Hor along the route to the Red Sea, to go around Edom. But the people grew impatient on the way; they spoke against God and against Moses, and said, "Why have you brought us up out of Egypt to die in the desert? There is no bread! There is no water! And we detest this miserable food!" Then the LORD sent venomous snakes among them; they bit the people and many Israelites died. The people came to Moses and said, "We sinned when we spoke against the LORD and against you. Pray that the LORD will take the snakes away from us." So Moses prayed for the people. The LORD said to Moses, "Make a snake and put it up on a pole; anyone who is bitten can look at it and live." So Moses made a bronze snake and put it up on a pole. Then when anyone was bitten by a snake and looked at the bronze snake, he lived. (Num 21:4-9)

This event in the Exodus foreshadowed the Cross of Christ. Jesus said, just as the people who looked at the bronze snake would live, so would it be true for those who looked to Christ on the cross.

When Christ was lifted up, anyone who looked at Him and believed in Him would have eternal life. *Just as Moses lifted up the snake in the desert, so the Son of Man must be lifted up, that everyone who believes in him may have eternal life. (John 3:14-15)*

Another important aspect of the cross was its relation to the sacrificial system which God instituted among the Israelites. One aspect of the sacrificial system was the sin offering, which was required for sins for which there was no possible restitution (Lev 4:5-13; 6:24-30). If the offering was accompanied by repentance, divine forgiveness was given (Num 15:30). The forgiveness of sin was represented by the blood smeared on the horns of the altar of incense and poured out at the base of the altar. Death, the penalty for all sin, was inflicted on the sacrificial animal. In that way, the guilt for the worshiper's sin was transferred symbolically to the animal through the laying on of the offerer's hands.

The *good news* from God was that the *new covenant* would be ratified by the blood, shed by Jesus Christ, the pure Paschal Lamb of God, who is the only begotten Son of the Father.

The next day John saw Jesus coming toward him and said, "Look, the Lamb of God, who takes away the sin of the world!" (John 1:29-30)

In the Passover meal, which Christians celebrate as the Eucharist (Thanksgiving), Christ told His disciples His blood of the new covenant was poured out for many for the forgiveness of sins.

While they were eating, Jesus took bread, gave thanks and broke it, and gave it to his disciples, saying, "Take and eat; this is my body." Then he took the cup, gave thanks and offered it to them, saying, "Drink from it, all of you. This is my [Christ] blood of the [new] covenant, which is poured out for many for the forgiveness of sins. I tell you, I will not drink of this fruit of the vine from now on until that day when I drink it anew with you in my Father's kingdom." (Matt 26:26-29)

Further, the Cross of Christ was also foreshadowed by the death and resuscitation of Lazarus (John 11:1-15). There are two significant truths regarding Lazarus. *First,* we see the authority of God over life and death. *Second,* the raising of Lazarus was a symbolic foreshadowing of the resurrection of Christ. However, in the case of Lazarus, his death and return to life was a resuscitation for Lazarus would die physically again.

This is in contrast to the death and resurrection of Jesus Christ.

The Cross of Christ is *good news* for the world.

The glory of the resurrection of Christ is the next stage of the *gospel of Christ.*

Tenth: The Resurrection of Christ: Eternal Life for the Righteous

The resurrection of Christ is prophesized and fulfilled throughout the Scripture.

Therefore my heart is glad and my tongue rejoices; my body also will rest secure, because you will not abandon me [your Holy One] to the grave, nor will you let your Holy One see decay. (Psa 16:9-10)

But God will redeem my life from the grave; he will surely take me to himself. (Psa 49:15)

The angel said to the women, "Do not be afraid, for I know that you are looking for Jesus, who was crucified. He is not here; he has risen, just as he said. Come and see the place where he lay. Then go quickly and tell his disciples: 'He has risen from the dead and is going ahead of you into Galilee. There you will see him.' Now I have told you." (Matt 28:5-7)

After his suffering, he showed himself to these men and gave many convincing proofs that he was alive. He appeared to them over a period of forty days and spoke about the kingdom of God. (Acts 1:3)

Paul, a servant of Christ Jesus, called to be an apostle and set apart for the gospel of God—the gospel he promised beforehand through his prophets in the Holy Scriptures regarding his Son, who as to his human nature was a descendant of David, and who through the Spirit of holiness was declared with power to be the Son of God by his resurrection from the dead: Jesus Christ our Lord. (Rom 1:1-4)

Further confirmation of this truth is found in Matthew 12:40-42, John 2:19-22, and Hebrews 13:20-21.

Christ came to die for the sins of the world, but God raised Him from the dead. As fully human and fully divine, He died physically; but, the divine Son of God did not die spiritually.

The resurrection of the Son of God is *good news* for the world.

After His resurrection and ascension, He will come again as King of kings and Lord of lords to execute judgment and rule the world.

Christ will come again.

That is the promise of Revelation 22:7, 12, and 20.

Behold, I [Christ] am coming soon! My reward is with me, and I will give to everyone according to what he has done. (Rev 22:12)

After the resurrection and ascension of Christ, we witness the promised coming of the Spirit.

Eleventh: The Coming of the Holy Spirit

The promise of the Spirit, made through the prophet Joel, will be fulfilled through Jesus Christ, who would fulfill three divine purposes.

John 16:8, 13, 14, When he [the Spirit] comes, he will convict the world of guilt in regard to sin and righteousness and judgment:…But when he, the Spirit of truth, comes, he will guide you into all truth. He will bring glory to me by taking from what is mine and making it known to you.

Further, Christ, just before His ascension, announced that His disciples will receive power to equip them to be His witnesses to the ends of the earth.

But you [Christ's disciples] will receive power when the Holy Spirit comes on you; and you will be my witnesses in Jerusalem, and in all Judea and Samaria, and to the ends of the earth. (Acts 1:8)

The promise of the Spirit was given; the promise was fulfilled.

Now, Christians, led by the Spirit, walk by the Spirit. In this way, Christians become a new creation (Gal 6:15). Further, Christians live in the power of the Spirit until the Second Coming of Christ.

That gospel message, we now address.

Twelfth, Christ's Second Coming

The Scriptures emphasize that Christ will come twice: first, as the Suffering Servant (Isaiah 53); second as the King of kings and Lord of lords (Rev 19:16).

The Old Testament contains many passages prophesying the Second Coming of Christ. Consider the following.

For to us a child is born, to us a son is given, and the government will be on his shoulders. And he will be called Wonderful Counselor, Mighty God, Everlasting Father, Prince of Peace. Of the increase of his government and peace there will be no end. He will reign on David's throne and over his kingdom, establishing and upholding it with justice and righteousness from that time on and forever. The zeal of the LORD Almighty will accomplish this. (Isa 9:6-7)

In my vision at night I looked, and there before me was one like a son of man, coming with the clouds of heaven. He approached the Ancient of Days [God] and was led into his presence. He was given authority, glory and sovereign power; all peoples, nations and men of every language worshiped him. His dominion is an everlasting dominion that will not pass away, and his kingdom is one that will never be destroyed. (Dan 7:13-14)

In like manner, the New Testament speaks of the fulfillment of these Old Testament prophecies.

When the Son of Man comes in his glory, and all the angels with him, he will sit on his throne in heavenly glory. (Matt 25:31)

And if I go and prepare a place for you, I will come back and take you to be with me that you also may be where I am. (John 14:3)

At the ascension of Christ, we find this promise in the Book of Acts: two men, dressed in white, spoke to His disciples.

They [His disciples] were looking intently up into the sky as he was going, when suddenly two men dressed in white stood beside them. "Men of Galilee," they said, "why do you stand here looking into the sky? This same Jesus, who has been taken from you into heaven, will come back in the same way you have seen him go into heaven." (Acts 1:10-11)

The *good news* is that, at His Second Coming, Christ will take us to be with Him. Further, His dominion will be an everlasting dominion that will not pass away. In that dominion, love, justice, and righteousness will mark His eternal reign. When Christ comes again, the Scriptures predict a general resurrection of all people. This is consistent with the prophecy in Daniel 12:1-4.

His return will establish the basis for the Eternal Kingdom.

Thirteenth: The Eternal Kingdom

How great are his signs, how mighty his wonders! His kingdom is an eternal kingdom; his dominion endures from generation to generation. (Dan 4:3)

For if you do these things, you will never fall, and you will receive a rich welcome into the eternal kingdom of our Lord and Savior Jesus Christ. (2 Peter 1:10-11)

The eternal kingdom, prophesized in Daniel, will be established, leading to the general resurrection.

Fourteenth: The General Resurrection

Not only will Christ return, which is good news, but everyone shall be resurrected; everyone shall stand before the Great White

Throne; everyone shall face the Final Judgment; everyone will have eternal life, some to everlasting life and others to shame and everlasting contempt.

At that time Michael, the great prince who protects your people, will arise. There will be a time of distress such as has not happened from the beginning of nations until then. But at that time your people — everyone whose name is found written in the book — will be delivered. Multitudes who sleep in the dust of the earth will awake: some to everlasting life, others to shame and everlasting contempt. Those who are wise will shine like the brightness of the heavens, and those who lead many to righteousness, like the stars forever and ever. But you, Daniel, close up and seal the words of the scroll until the time of the end. Many will go here and there to increase knowledge. (Dan 12:1-4)

So, everyone will be resurrected and everyone will have eternal life; some to eternal life with God and some to everlasting contempt and damnation.

The Old Testament teaches a resurrection by the use of terms, such as *sleep,* to indicate physical death. Many times, the phrase, used of death, is to *sleep with their ancestors.* However, the meaning is clear. If a person is to *sleep* in death, it indicates that there will be an awaking from that sleep, which is termed a resurrection.

Look on me and answer, O LORD my God. Give light to my eyes, or I will sleep in death; (Psa 13:3)

You [God] sweep men away in the sleep of death; they are like the new grass of the morning — (Psa 90:5)

The New Testament consistently teaches hope in the resurrection of the believer based upon the resurrection of Christ as the *"firstborn from the dead"* (1 Cor 15:20-28; Col 1:18; 1 Thess 4:14-18; 1 Peter 1:3-5).

In the same way that our baptism is modeled on that of Jesus Christ, our resurrection is also modeled on His resurrection. As He was raised from the dead and knows the fruit of eternal life, so shall all who have faith in Him and whose name is written in the Book of Life.

We must remember that all people will experience the resurrection, which will lead to the Final Judgment.

But Christ has indeed been raised from the dead, the firstfruits of those who have fallen asleep. For since death came through a man, the resurrection of the dead comes also through a man. For as in Adam all die, so in Christ all will be made alive. But each in his own turn: Christ, the firstfruits; then, when he comes, those who belong to him. Then the end will come, when he hands over the kingdom to God the Father after he has destroyed all dominion, authority and power. (1 Cor 15:20-22)

Resurrection is expressed in terms, such as a *transformed body* (Phil 3:21), a *new dwelling* (2 Cor 5:2), and *new clothing* (2 Cor 5:4; Rev 6:11). The New Testament also contrasts resurrection to life with resurrection to judgment (John 5:29; Acts 24:15).

Do not be amazed at this, for a time is coming when all who are in their graves will hear his voice and come out — those who have done good will rise to live, and those who have done evil will rise to be condemned. (John 5:28-29)

It is clear that all people will be resurrected, some to *life*, some to be *condemned*. In the same way, all people will experience eternal life; some to everlasting life, and some to everlasting contempt.

I [Paul] have the same hope in God as these men, that there will be a resurrection of both the righteous and the wicked. (Acts 24:15)

There is a similar contrast behind the statements in Revelation 20 about *the first resurrection* (20:5) and *the second death* (20:14).

They came to life and reigned with Christ a thousand years. (The rest of the dead did not come to life until the thousand years were ended.) This is the first resurrection. Blessed and holy are those who have part in the first resurrection. The second death has no power over them, but they will be priests of God and of Christ and will reign with him for a thousand years. (Rev 20:4-6)

Then death and Hades were thrown into the lake of fire. The lake of fire is the second death. If anyone's name was not found written in the book of life, he was thrown into the lake of fire. (Rev 20:14-15)

We next turn to the Final Judgment.

Fifthteenth: The Final Judgment: Reward and Punishment

In Scripture, the Final Judgment results in the ultimate separation of good and evil at the end of the age. The precise time of this judgment is appointed by God (Acts 17:31), and it remains unknown to man (Matt 24:36). The return of the Lord to earth, the resurrection of the dead, and the Final Judgment, together with the end of the world--all these may be thought of as belonging to a single set of events at the end of time.

When the Son of Man comes in his glory, and all the angels with him, he will sit on his throne in heavenly glory. All the nations will be gathered before him, and he will separate the people one from another as a shepherd separates the sheep from the goats. He will put the sheep on his right and the goats on his left. Then the King will say to those on his right, "Come, you who are blessed by my Father; take your inheritance, the kingdom prepared for you since the creation of the world." (Matt 25:31-35)

With God, His Final Judgment results in the conquest and victory of good over evil. God judges His people and their actions according to His standards. There are many Old and New Testament passages that describe the reason and the character of this final Judgment. Consider John 5:24 as representative.

I tell you the truth, whoever hears my [Christ] word and believes him [God] who sent me has eternal life and will not be condemned; he has crossed over from death to life. I tell you the truth, a time is coming and has now come when the dead will hear the voice of the Son of God and those who hear will live. For as the Father has life in himself, so he has granted the Son to have life in himself. And he has given him authority to judge because he is the Son of Man. (John 5:24-27)

From earliest times it has been recognized that God Himself is the Judge of mankind (Gen 18:25), and that He has the power and wisdom to judge with righteousness, truth, and justice (Ps 96:13; 98:9). The final judgment is given specifically to God's Son (John 5:22; Acts 17:31) to conclude His work as Mediator, Deliverer of His people from sin, and Destroyer of God's enemies. God's people will be associated with Christ in the exercise of this Final Judgment (1 Cor 6:2-3; Rev 20:4).

The Final Judgment will be comprehensive in scope; it will include all people and all nations from the beginning of the world to the end of history (Matt 25:31-46; Rom 14:10-12), as well as fallen angels (2 Peter 2:4). Those who trust in the Lord, repent of sin, and walk in His ways will not be condemned but will enter into eternal life (Ps 1).

The purpose of the Final Judgment is to reveal the glory of God through the justification of the godly and the condemnation of the ungodly (2 Thess 1:3-10).

The death of Jesus Christ is unique among these judgments of history. Through His death, God paid the judgment price demanded by mankind's sin. The death and resurrection of Jesus are the foundations on which sinners are saved (Isa 53:5) through their trust in Him as Savior and Lord.

The *Book of Life* contains the names of the righteous. This *Book of Life* was first mentioned by Moses, who prayed that God would not blot him out of God's book rather than dooming his fellow Israelites (Ex 32:32-33). This concept likely arose from the practice of registering people by genealogy (Neh 7:5, 64) and keeping a record of priests and Levites. (Neh 12:22-23)

The *Book of Life* identifies the citizens of the New Jerusalem.

At the end of the age (Rev 20:11-15), those whose names are not written in the Book of Life will be *cast into the lake of fire* (Rev 20:15). But those whose names appear in that Book (Rev 21:27) will enter the New Jerusalem, as residents of the City of God.

Nothing impure will ever enter it [the New Jerusalem], nor will anyone who does what is shameful or deceitful, but only those whose names are written in the Lamb's book of life. (Rev 21:27)

The Final Judgment will determine the residents of the New Heaven and the New Earth and the New Jerusalem, the City of God.

We now reach the conclusion of the *gospel of Christ*, as eternity prepares for the New Heaven, the New Earth, and the New Jerusalem.

Sixteenth: The New Heaven, the New Earth, the New Jerusalem (Rev 21:1-4)

We now come to the end of the gospel message. We come to the New Heaven, the New Earth and the New Jerusalem. The ultimate good news is that those whose names are written in the *Book of Life* will live in that divine kingdom, under the rule of the righteous King, Jesus Christ.

See what the Apostle John was privileged to see.

Then I [the Apostle John] saw a new heaven and a new earth, for the first heaven and the first earth had passed away, and there was no longer any sea. I saw the Holy City, the new Jerusalem, coming down out of heaven from God, prepared as a bride beautifully dressed for her husband. And I heard a loud voice from the throne saying, "Now the dwelling of God is with men, and he will live with them. They will be his people, and God himself will be with them and be their God. He will wipe every tear from their eyes. There will be no more death or mourning or crying or pain, for the old order of things has passed away." He who was seated on the throne [Christ] said, "I am making everything new!" (Rev 21:1-5)

The original heavens foreshadow the New Heaven.

The original earth foreshadows the New Earth.

The original Jerusalem foreshadows the New Jerusalem.

Christ said: *I am making everything new! (Rev 22:5, 7, 20)*

The righteous share eternity in the *new.*

And so this example of the gospel message is concluded.

Sixteen promises were considered; their fulfillment was seen; new promises are on the horizon.

We have seen the following: *The Covenant with Abraham; The Promise of the Spirit; The New Covenant for the Forgiveness of Sin; The Promise of the Everlasting Kingdom; The Promise of the Messiah; The Promise of Eternal Life; The Incarnation; The New Birth; The Cross of Christ; The Resurrection of Christ; Eternal Life; The Coming of the Holy Spirit; Christ's Second Coming; The Kingdom of God; The Eternal Kingdom; The General Resurrection: The Final Judgment: Reward and Punishment; The New Heaven, The New Earth, the New Jerusalem: the New Creation.*

This is all good news; some has occurred; much lies in the future.

However, the conclusion is certain. God's holy purposes will be fulfilled.

So we summarize.

The gospel message is this: God first announced the gospel to Abraham, because of his obedience and faithfulness. God also made a covenant with Abraham that all the nations would be blessed (justified) through his offspring, who will be the Christ. Next, God made a promise through the prophet, Joel, that God would send forth His Holy Spirit, so that all of His people would have all power to accomplish every divine purpose. Further, God proclaimed through the prophet Jeremiah, that forgiveness of sins would be made available to those who repented of sins and had faith in God. Further, God decreed that His Kingdom would be an everlasting Kingdom. This was all a prelude to the Incarnation, the birth of His only begotten Son, who would come to die for the sins of the world and ratify all previous covenants and promises. The birth of Christ was a forerunner to the death of Christ on the Cross, by which forgiveness of sins and redemption and reconciliation with God will result. The death of Christ led to the remarkable physical and spiritual resurrection of God where Christ is now seated at the right hand of God. As was promised, Christ will come again as King of kings and Lord of Lords. As Christ was resurrected, so shall all people be resurrected. The resurrection will lead to the Final Judgment, at which time, everyone will receive just reward or just punishment. The resurrection is the foundation of eternal life, for all those who have received Him and believed in His name. At the completion of the Final Judgment, all things will be made new. This earth and the present heavens will disappear, and there will be a New Heaven and a New Earth and a New Jerusalem. The final portion of the good news is this: everyone whose name is written in the Lamb's Book of Life will spend eternity with God in His heavenly city, the New Jerusalem. Everything will be made new.

This is the theological summary of the gospel of Christ.

While this explanation of the theology of the gospel of Christ is important, we must recognize that Scripture contains many other examples of the gospel that deserve our attention. Since the gospel means *good news from God,* we would acknowledge that there are many examples of such good news. For our purposes, I have selected the following three:

- The Gospel according to John: John 3:16-21
- Paul's Gospel summary: Romans, chapters 1-8
- The Epistle to the Romans: 10:8-13

The Gospel according to John: John 3:16-21

16 For God so loved the world that he gave his one and only Son, that whoever believes in him shall not perish but have eternal life. 17 For God did not send his Son into the world to condemn the world, but to save the world through him. 18 Whoever believes in him is not condemned, but whoever does not believe stands condemned already because he has not believed in the name of God's one and only Son. 19 This is the verdict: Light has come into the world, but men loved darkness instead of light because their deeds were evil. 20 Everyone who does evil hates the light, and will not come into the light for fear that his deeds will be exposed. 21 But whoever lives by the truth comes into the light, so that it may be seen plainly that what he [Christ] has done has been done through God. (John 3:16-21)

There are many biblical truths in this gospel passage. First, there is the evidence of God's great love for the world. God gave His only Son that whoever believed in Him would have eternal life. God gave so that we would have eternal life with Him, because of our faith in His Son. Second, God did not send His Son to condemn the world but to save the world through His Son. There is no condemnation for those who are in Christ; however, everyone who does not believe in the Son stands condemned already. Third, God has sent His Light, His Son, into the world, and there is now a choice between the Light and the darkness. There is an alternative. The question is: which will each person choose? Many choose the darkness because their deeds are evil: if, in the Light, their evil deeds will be exposed.

However, those who live by the truth come into the Light, and they see that which Jesus Christ has done has been done through God. The Hand of God is evident in the mission of His Son.

God sent His Son to redeem the world and provide forgiveness of sins to all who receive and believe in Him.

This gospel passage has been shared with the world since the beginning of time. It is a great passage to use in explaining to unbelievers the love of God and the atoning sacrifice of His Son for the redemption and reconciliation of the world. It explains the depth of divine love; it defines the evil in the world; it identifies the choice that is placed before each individual.

This proclamation calls for the recognition of sin, repentance from sin, the acceptance of Christ, and the eternal life which God offers to all who accept His Son as both Savior and Lord. Above all, it calls for a personal relationship with God the Father of all.

Paul's Gospel Summary: Romans, chapters 1-8

This example summarizes the theology of the gospel, announced through the apostle Paul in his Epistle to the Romans: chapters 1-8. This is Paul's sixth epistle and was most likely written about 56 AD, about seven years after his first epistle which was to the Galatians (49 AD). Paul's 13 epistles are the first written New Testament documents and thereby represent the first written expressions of the gospel of Christ.

There are few books in all the Scriptures that have commanded the attention of this letter. There are many who have been converted and regenerated by the power and simplicity of this gospel message. Those who attest to the majesty of this text include Augustine, Martin Luther, John Calvin, William Tyndale, John and Charles Wesley, George Whitefield, Karl Barth, and many others. Martin Luther called it *truly the purest and grandest of all versions of the gospel...every Christian should occupy himself with it every day.* John Calvin wrote: *if we have gained a true understanding of this epistle, we have an open door to all the most profound treasures of Scripture.* William Tyndale, the father of English Bible translators, wrote: *it is the principal and most excellent part of the New Testament and most pure glad tidings....and also a light and a way into the whole Scripture.* In recent times, one of the most significant theological publications of the twentieth century was Karl Barth's commentary on Paul's Epistle to the Romans, published in August 1918. In his preface, Barth wrote: *the reader will detect for himself that it has been written with a joyful sense of discovery. The mighty voice of Paul was new to me, and, if to me, then no doubt to many others. And now that my work is finished, I perceive that much remains which I have not yet heard.*

The impact that this epistle had on these men is only a glimpse into the tremendous effect that it has had on the Christian landscape.

In his presentation of the gospel, Paul developed two major themes, both interwoven. The first is *justification of guilty sinners by God's grace alone in Christ alone through faith alone,* independent of status or works. This is the most humbling and revealing of all Christian truths. Paul is consistently true to this basic theme, repeating this same message in the Epistle to the Ephesians: *For it is by grace you have been saved, through faith — and this not from yourselves, it is the gift of God— not by works, so that no one can boast. (Eph 2:8-9)*

No one better understood the true essence of the theology of Paul, *salvation by grace alone through faith alone,* than did Augustine and Martin Luther.

The second major theme is the *redefinition of the people of God,* no longer according to descent, culture, the law or circumcision— but according to faith in Jesus Christ. So there is no difference between Jew or Gentile, regarding the fact of their sin or guilt or in Christ's offer and gift of salvation and eternal life.

Paul presents a gospel of freedom: freedom from sin, freedom from the Law, freedom from the sting of death, and freedom to be the *new creation (Gal 6:15)* for which we were created.

Those who have been set free by the Cross of Christ enjoy new power and new liberty.

Its central message is the death and resurrection of Jesus Christ.

Those who receive Him, who believe in Him, who accept Him as Savior and Lord, who serve Him as faithful disciples, they will share in the general resurrection yet to come.

The Bible has many rich statements that express the gospel of Christ. The purpose is always that, by the gospel, salvation is the free gift of God, offered by the grace of God. Our response to this free gift is faith, which is the *assurance of things hoped for, the conviction of things not seen. (Heb 11:1* RSV)

The gospel is the good news of salvation. God, by His grace and in His holy righteousness, has redeemed us through the Cross of Christ. Salvation is through faith alone in Christ alone. No one comes to the Father except through the Son (John 14:6).

In summary, the gospel is the divine message that God the Father sent God the Son to save sinners, to redeem the world by

His gracious sacrifice on the cross, to die for the forgiveness of sins, so that we, who receive Him and believe in His name, might be reconciled to God the Father and become His children and His righteousness.

Paul closed his statement of the gospel with this great affirmation.

What, then, shall we say in response to this? If God is for us, who can be against us? He who did not spare his own Son, but gave him up for us all — how will he not also, along with him, graciously give us all things? Who will bring any charge against those whom God has chosen? It is God who justifies. Who is he that condemns? Christ Jesus, who died — more than that, who was raised to life — is at the right hand of God and is also interceding for us. Who shall separate us from the love of Christ? Shall trouble or hardship or persecution or famine or nakedness or danger or sword? As it is written: "For your sake we face death all day long; we are considered as sheep to be slaughtered."

No, in all these things we are more than conquerors through him who loved us. For I am convinced that neither death nor life, neither angels nor demons, neither the present nor the future, nor any powers, neither height nor depth, nor anything else in all creation, will be able to separate us from the love of God that is in Christ Jesus our Lord. (Rom 8:31-39)

There is so much more in these eight chapters that warrant our attention. For me to discuss such great theological themes would demand a commentary to rival that of Karl Barth and many others. Therefore, the reader is directed to the many commentaries available to gain that fresh insight into the gospel of Christ as presented by the apostle Paul.

The Epistle to the Romans: Romans 10:8-13

In this passage, the apostle Paul states our confession of Christ and the result of that confession. This good news contains the basis of salvation to those who acknowledge the faith to stand firm in belief and conviction of the power in the name of Jesus Christ.

8 But what does it say? "The word is near you; it is in your mouth and in your heart," that is, the word of faith we are proclaiming: 9 That if you confess with your mouth, "Jesus is Lord," and believe in your heart that God raised him from the dead, you will be saved. 10 For it is with your heart that you believe and are justified, and it is with your mouth that you confess and are saved. 11 As the Scripture says, "Anyone who trusts in him will never be put to shame." 12 For there is no difference between Jew and Gentile — the same Lord is Lord of all and richly blesses all who call on him, 13 for, "Everyone who calls on the name of the Lord will be saved."

And so we conclude our examination of the gospel of Christ.

The message of the gospel is this: God loves us, has delivered us, has redeemed us, has forgiven us, has protected us, has provided for us, has equipped us, and has empowered us. That is the good news, the gospel of Christ.

Chapter 8

The gospel is **the power of God** for the salvation of everyone who believes (Rom 1:16)

For God so loved the world that he gave his one and only Son, that whoever believes in him shall not perish but have eternal life. (John 3:16)

Believe in the Lord Jesus, and you will be saved — you and your household (Acts 16:31)

I am not ashamed of the gospel, because it is the power of God for the salvation of everyone who believes: first for the Jew, then for the Gentile. (Rom 1:16)

That if you confess with your mouth, "Jesus is Lord," and believe in your heart that God raised him from the dead, you will be saved. (Rom 10:9)

For it is by grace you have been saved, through faith — and this not from yourselves, it is the gift of God. (Eph 2:8)

Jews demand miraculous signs and Greeks look for wisdom, but we preach Christ crucified: a stumbling block to Jews and foolishness to Gentiles, but to those whom God has called, both Jews and Greeks, Christ the power of God and the wisdom of God. For the foolishness of God is wiser than man's wisdom, and the weakness of God is stronger than man's strength. (1 Cor 1:22-25)

Paul now defines the gospel in a concise manner. His definition is: *the power of God for the salvation of everyone who believes.*

Therefore, in the next three chapters, we will examine the fullness of Paul's theology.

So Paul directs our attention first to the *power of God.*

It is interesting that this term, the *power of God,* is mentioned only ten times in the Bible. However, the entire Bible is a witness to the *power of God,* demonstrated throughout divine and human history.

As expressions of His power, consider the passages at the beginning of this chapter.

From Romans 1:16-17, we learn that the *power of God is the basis of salvation.*

From I Corinthians 1:18-19, we learn that the *cross* is the ultimate witness of the *power of God.*

From I Corinthians 1:22-25, we learn that *Christ Himself is the power of God.*

The power of God is for the salvation of the world; that power is demonstrated through Jesus Christ as the Mediator and the Agent of our salvation.

The following subjects will be examined in our discussion of the power of God: 1. *The Power of God: Summary Definition: 2. Christ: the Revelation of the Power of God: 3. God's Revelation of His Power in Creation, Exodus, Cross, Kingdom: 4. His Power as shown in the Faithfulness in the Lives of His People: 5. His Power as shown in the Transformation in the Lives of His People.*

1. *The Power of God: Summary Definition*

As stated earlier, Creation, the Bible, history (divine and secular), and Jesus Christ are supreme examples of the *power of God.*

God has *power* which is the reflection of His sovereignty and authority. His power is totally consistent with His authority. His power is unlimited, without restraint, and independent of any other authority or power. It is absolute power because it reflects His divine authority. As His authority is absolute, so is His power; His power is shown in both the physical and spiritual realms.

The *power of God* is shown in what God Himself does: by the Flood, by the Exodus, by the Cross, by the transformation in the lives of His people, and the victory that the saints achieve under the Lordship of Jesus Christ.

The *power of God*, His omnipotence, is exclusively an attribute of God and essential to the perfection of His being. His omnipotence is self-proclaimed, as in Gen 17:1; Ex 15:11-12; Deut 3:24; Ps 62:11; 65:6; 147:5; Jer 32:17; Matt 6:13; 19:26; Eph 3:20; Rev 19:6. He has authority and power to do everything that is consistent with His holy, just, and perfect nature (Matt 23:19; Heb 6:18). The power of God is set before us in the Scriptures in connection with His work of Creation (Gen 1:1; Rom 1:20), His work of upholding the world (Heb 1:3), the redemption and reconciliation of mankind (Luke 1:35, 37; Eph 1:19), the working of signs and miracles (Luke 9:43), the conversion of sinners (1 Cor 2:5; 2 Cor 4:7), of being found by a people who did not seek Him, and the complete accomplishment of the great purpose of His kingdom (Matt 6:13; 13:31-32; 1 Peter 1:5; 1 Cor 15:1; Rev 19:6).

The preaching of the gospel is accompanied by the power of the Holy Spirit (1 Cor 2:4; 1 Thess 1:5). Signs and miracles, as *mighty works*, are denoted by His *powers*. The end of the age will occur when God takes to Himself His great power and reigns (Rev 11:17).

We give thanks to you, Lord God Almighty, the One who is and who was, because you have taken your great power and have begun to reign. (Rev 11:17)

So what is the *power of God*? It is the righteous, just, holy, and divine power that is the result of righteous and divine authority. As divine, God has full authority and power over all things supernatural and natural, visible and invisible.

The power of God is without limits; it is a power that is totally under control; it is a power that is used only for good. However,

His power is also expressed in His wrath against sin. God has the power to control and restrict evil.

His greatest power is His love, expressed through His Son and revealed through the Holy Spirit.

It is the power to create the universe and all that is within it.

It is the power to transform people, the universe, and all that is in the universe.

It is the power to raise the dead and the power to heal all that are afflicted.

It is the power to control what God has created.

It is the power to forgive sins, which are acknowledged, confessed, and repented.

It is omnipotence in everything and everywhere, the visible and the invisible.

This word, power, is indicative of might, strength, force. God's power is capable of anything, and it has the ability to perform anything. There are no limits and no restrictions.

God has the inherent ability to affect all the divine and natural purposes. God's power, wisely used, provides the fullness of all good. God's power is intrinsic excellence.

God has the power to exercise His full authority. In that way, power and authority are mutually inclusive in the will and purpose of God.

Power is attributed preeminently to God (1 Chron 29:11; Job 26:14; Ps 66:7; 145:11; Rev 7:12, etc.). The supreme manifestation of the power, as of the wisdom and love of God, is in redemption and reconciliation (1 Cor 1:18, 24). The preaching of the gospel is accompanied by the *power* of the Holy Spirit (1 Cor 2:4; 1 Thess 1:5, etc.). Signs and miracles, often defined as *mighty works*, are denoted by the term *powers* (Matt 11:21, 23). The end of all divine history will occur when God takes to Him His omnipotence and reigns (Rev 11:17).

We give thanks to you, Lord God Almighty, the One who is and who was, because you have taken your great power and have begun to reign. The nations were angry; and your wrath has come. The time has come for judging the dead, and for rewarding your servants the prophets and your saints and those who reverence your name, both small and great — and for destroying those who destroy the earth. (Rev 11:17-18)

The single most important definition is: *Christ as the power of God* (I Cor 1:24).

On that basis, when we speak of the *power of God*, that equates to the *power of Christ*.

This fundamental truth is the basis for all else that is rightfully claimed regarding the *power of God*.

Further, when we speak of God in these terms, we are referring to the Triune God, who is Father, Son, and Spirit. The emphasis of Scripture is that the Father has given all authority and power to the Son, so that the will of the Godhead will be accomplished. Since the Father has given the Son all authority and power, the gospel is given through the Son.

So when we speak of the power of God, we are really speaking of His power which is given by the Father and is fully in His Son, the Christ.

For he [God] "has put everything under his feet." Now when it says that "everything" has been put under him, it is clear that this does not include God himself, who put everything under Christ. When he [Christ] has done this, then the Son himself will be made subject to him who put everything under him, so that God may be all in all. (1 Cor 15:27-28)

Consider other passages that describe the *power of God*.

Proclaim the power of God, whose majesty is over Israel, whose power is in the skies. You are awesome, O God, in your sanctuary; the God of Israel gives power and strength to his people. Praise be to God! (Psa 68:34-35)

For the message of the cross is foolishness to those who are perishing, but to us who are being saved it is the power of God. (1 Cor 1:18)

So do not be ashamed to testify about our Lord, or ashamed of me his prisoner. But join with me in suffering for the gospel, by the power of God, who has saved us and called us to a holy life — not because of anything we have done but because of his own purpose and grace. (2 Tim 1:8-9)

And the twenty-four elders, who were seated on their thrones before God, fell on their faces and worshiped God, saying: "We give thanks to you, Lord God Almighty, the One who is and who was, because you have taken your great power and have begun to reign. The nations were angry; and your wrath has come. The time has come for judging the dead, and for rewarding your servants the prophets and your saints and those who reverence your name, both small and great — and for destroying those who destroy the earth." Then God's temple in heaven was opened, and within his temple was seen the ark of his covenant. And there came flashes of lightning, rumblings, peals of thunder, an earthquake and a great hailstorm. (Rev 11:16-19)

One of the great messages in Scripture is in Luke 1:37: *with God, nothing is impossible.*

Nothing is impossible because God is omnipotent.

Conversely, with God, everything that He decrees is not only possible: it is certain to occur.

His gospel is disclosed and sent forth into the world by His power. There is no gospel except that in which the power of God is evident.

His power is to fulfill that which He determines to do: *so is my word that goes out from my mouth: It will not return to me empty, but will accomplish what I desire and achieve the purpose for which I sent it. (Isa 55:11)*

God's word *will accomplish what He desires and achieve the purpose for which He sent it.*

Nothing can prevent the full expression of His power.

Without reservation, God has divine sovereignty, authority and power. God is omnipotent.

2. Christ: The Revelation of the Power of God:

Three passages, John 1:1-5; Romans 11:36; and Colossians 1:15-20, define Christ as the living Word of God and as the *power of God*.

In the beginning was the Word, and the Word was with God, and the Word was God. He was with God in the beginning. Through him all things were made; without him nothing was made that has been made. In him was life, and that life was the light of men. The light shines in the darkness, but the darkness has not understood it. (John 1:1-5)

This passage describes Christ as the *power of God*; Christ was from the beginning; Christ was/is always with God; Christ is God. Through Him were all things made; He is life and that life was the light of men. The light shown in the darkness (the world), but the world did not understand the significance of the light.

The second passage, Romans 11:36, amplifies the first.

For from him [Christ] and through him and to him are all things. To him be the glory forever! Amen. (Rom 11:36)

Here is further testimony that all things are *from Him*, come *through Him* and *belong to Him*. Because of that supremacy, to Him is ascribed all glory and majesty and power.

The third passage, Colossians 1:15-20, adds new understanding to the *power of God* as revealed in Christ. This passage also reveals the supremacy of Christ in all things.

He [Christ] is the image of the invisible God, the firstborn over all creation. For by him all things were created: things in heaven and on earth, visible and invisible, whether thrones or powers or rulers or authorities; all things were created by him and for him. He is before all things, and in him all things hold together. And he is the head of the body, the church; he is the beginning and the firstborn from among the dead, so that in everything he might have the supremacy. For God was pleased to have all his fullness dwell in him, and through him to reconcile to himself all things, whether things on earth or things in heaven, by making peace through his blood, shed on the cross. (Col 1:15-20)

Christ is the image of the invisible God, and all things were created by Him and for Him. He has supremacy, the power of God, in all things. He is the Head of the Assembly of God's people; and, as the church, we are to submit to His authority and power. He will redeem and reconcile all things, whether on earth or in heaven, to Himself by making peace through His blood, shed on the cross. In this passage, the Crucified One becomes the King of all kings and Lord of all lords.

Many other passages confirm the authority and power of Christ.

Then Jesus came to them [the disciples] and said, "All authority in heaven and on earth has been given to me." (Matt 28:18)

For in Christ all the fullness of the Deity lives in bodily form, and you have been given fullness in Christ, who is the head over every power and authority. (Col 2:9-10)

Then I heard a loud voice in heaven say: "Now have come the salvation and the power and the kingdom of our God, and the authority of his Christ." (Rev 12:10)

With the understanding of these passages, we accept Romans 1:16: *the gospel is the power of God for the salvation of everyone who believes.*

The power of God is equally the power of Christ.

In a Trinitarian sense, this is true because the Father had sent the Son, to bring about the salvation of all who believe; the Holy Spirit will lead all who believe out of darkness and into His marvelous light.

The Father has given the Son all authority and power. However, when the end of the age comes, then the Son will return that same authority and power to the Father.

Then the end will come, when he [Christ] hands over the kingdom to God the Father after he has destroyed all dominion, authority and power. For he [Christ] must reign until he has put all his enemies under his feet. The last enemy to be destroyed is death. For he "has put everything under his feet." Now when it says that "everything" has been put under him, it is clear that this does not include God himself, who put everything under Christ. When he has done this, then the Son himself will be made subject to him who put everything under him, so that God may be all in all. (1 Cor 15:24-28)

The reason my Father loves me is that I lay down my life — only to take it up again. No one takes it from me, but I lay it down of my own accord. I have authority to lay it down and authority to take it up again. This command I received from my Father. (John 10:17-18)

God has power to create, and He has power to destroy. He has power to control the destiny of the world, because it is His world, created under His sovereignty, by His authority, and sustained by His power.

He alone is sovereign; He alone has all authority; He alone has absolute power.

Let us next consider the Bible as the revelation of the power of God.

3. The Bible: God's Written Word as a Revelation of the power of God:

It is by His authority and His power that the Bible is ordained.

Does the written Word of God have power? Certainly. The written Word of God, the Bible, has power to instruct us for salvation through faith in Christ Jesus.

In exactly the same way, the gospel also instructs us regarding the resurrection and eternal life as true elements of salvation.

Christians acknowledge the truth that, by faith, God created the natural universe out of nothing. The writer of the Epistle to the Hebrews in the New Testament declared, By faith we understand that the world was framed by the word of God, so that the things which are seen were not made of things which are visible (Heb 11:3). God spoke and creation came into being. The breath of God accomplishes the purpose of God.

Since God created the universe, it is His and is designed to serve His purpose. As He shaped creation without any assistance, He will bring creation to its desired end without any assistance. No other power is needed to complete the process of creation and recreation. In the same way, no power can frustrate God in His purpose to complete the process started in creation and revealed in Scripture. Our hope rests in the sovereign power of Him who created the world and then re-created us through the saving power of His Son, Jesus Christ.

Consider next the sovereign power of God to sustain all that He created.

4. Upholding the World as a Revelation of the Power of God:

What God created, He will also sustain. He gives the Creation what is necessary for its existence and for every aspect of its future existence. The Creation is kept in complete order, until the coming of the New Heaven and the New Earth, with the New Jerusalem (Rev 21:1-4).

The Son is the radiance of God's glory and the exact representation of his being, sustaining all things by his powerful word (Heb 1:3)

5. Redemption of Mankind as a Revelation of the Power of God:

Redemption is the deliverance of a person in slavery to another by the payment of a price. In that respect, the person is redeemed. In the New Testament, redemption is a double process: it refers to freedom *from* slavery to sin, death, and the wrath of God and *to* freedom in Christ and reconciliation with God. This redemption is the result of Christ's sacrifice for the sins of the world.

Redemption teaches the world of two great truths; first, the seriousness of sins; second, the tremendous price that God Himself paid for the reconciliation of repentant sinners.

The New Testament emphasizes the tremendous cost of redemption: *the precious blood of Christ* (1 Pet 1:19; Eph 1:7), which is an atoning sacrifice, propitiation *by His blood* (Rom 3:25). Propitiation has two dimensions, as it defined Christ's roles in His death on the Cross. It relates to God and it relates to us as repentant sinners. First of all, it means His death for our sins; second, it means Christ's turning aside the wrath of God against our sins.

Believers are reminded of the *price* of their redemption; as such, this reminder is the motivation to encourage personal holiness (1 Cor 6:19-20; 1 Pet 1:13-19).

Do you not know that your body is a temple of the Holy Spirit, who is in you, whom you have received from God? You are not your own; you were bought at a price. Therefore honor God with your body. (1 Cor 6:19-20)

For you know that it was not with perishable things such as silver or gold that you were redeemed from the empty way of life handed down to you from your forefathers, but with the precious blood of Christ, a lamb without blemish or defect. He was chosen before the creation of the world, but was revealed in these last times for your sake. Through him you believe in God, who raised him from the dead and glorified him, and so your faith and hope are in God. (1 Pet 1:18-21)

These two passages contain great truths: *first,* your body is a temple of the Holy Spirit, whom you have received from God. *Second,* you are not your own; you belong to the one who has redeemed you. *Third,* the price for your redemption was not silver and gold: the price was far higher than that. *Fourth,* it required the blood of the Son of God to redeem us. *Fifth,* by the shedding of His blood, we have been reconciled to God.

I pray also that the eyes of your heart may be enlightened in order that you may know the hope to which he has called you, the riches of his glorious inheritance in the saints, and his incomparably great power for us who believe. That power is like the working of his mighty strength, which he exerted in Christ when he raised him from the dead and seated him at his right hand in the heavenly realms, far above all rule and authority, power and dominion, and every title that can be given, not only in the present age but also in the one to come. (Eph 1:18-21)

6. Signs: a Revelation of the Power of God:

Both the Old and New Testaments witness to the signs that God has done in and through His people. Signs, linked with both *wonders* and *miracles* (Acts 2:22; 2 Cor 12:12; Heb 2:4), point primarily to the Presence of God as witnessed through the ministry of Jesus and the apostles. The word, sign, occurs frequently in the Gospel of John, pointing to the deeper symbolic and spiritual meaning of the supernatural acts performed by Jesus Christ. Throughout the Bible, the true significance of a sign is understood only through faith.

Consider the mighty wonders that God performed through Moses and Aaron to secure the release of the Israelites from the hand of Pharaoh.

So I [God] will stretch out my hand and strike the Egyptians with all the wonders that I will perform among them. After that, he will let you go. (Exo 3:20)

Before all your people I [God] will do wonders never before done in any nation in all the world. The people you live among will see how awesome is the work that I, the Lord, will do for you. Obey what I command you today. (Exo 34:10-11)

And who is like your people Israel — the one nation on earth that God went out to redeem as a people for himself, and to make a name for himself, and to perform great and awesome wonders by driving out nations and their gods from before your people, whom you redeemed from Egypt? You have established your people Israel as your very own forever, and you, O LORD, have become their God. (2 Sam 7:23-24)

In the last days, God says, I will pour out my Spirit on all people....I will show wonders in the heaven above and signs on the earth below, blood and fire and billows of smoke. The sun will be turned to darkness and the moon to blood before the coming of the great and glorious day of the Lord. And everyone who calls on the name of the Lord will be saved. (Acts 2:17-21)

How great are his [God's] signs, how mighty his wonders! His kingdom is an eternal kingdom; his dominion endures from generation to generation. (Dan 4:3)

Consider the mighty signs fulfilled in Jesus Christ.

7. The signs of Jesus Christ: a Revelation of the Power of God

The Bible presents the teachings and witness of Jesus Christ into three distinct phases. The first phase consisted of performing many miraculous signs; the second phase consisted of direct statements, proclaiming His role and mission; the third phase consisted of parables.

In the first phase, Jesus performed many signs, of which six are recorded in the Gospel according to John. Jesus expected that the signs would authenticate His Presence as the Son of God. *This, the first of his miraculous signs [changing water into wine], Jesus performed at Cana in Galilee. He thus revealed his glory, and his disciples put their faith in him. (John 2:11).* The second sign: the healing of the Son of an Official (John 4:46-54); the third sign: the healing of the paralytic (John 5:1-21); the fourth sign: The Feeding of the 5,000 (John 6:1-14); the fifth sign: The Healing of the Blind Man (John 9:1-25); and the sixth sign: the raising of Lazarus (John 11:1-44).

The Apostle John also recorded: *Jesus did many other miraculous signs in the presence of his disciples, which are not recorded in this book. But these are written that you may believe that Jesus is the Christ, the Son of God, and that by believing you may have life in his name. (John 20:30-31)*

According to this passage, these supernatural and divine signs were given for two reasons: *first,* that the witnesses would believe that Jesus is the Christ, the Son of God; *second,* that, by believing, the witnesses would have life (salvation) in His name.

The second phase represented direct statements, the *I am* passages, which was the name of God, the great *I AM*, proclaimed to Moses (Exo 3:14). These passages relate to Christ's seven proclamations as: *the bread of life (Jn. 6:35); the light of the world (Jn. 8:21); the gate of the sheep (Jn 10:7); the good shepherd (Jn. 10:11); the resurrection and the life (Jn. 11:25); the way, the truth, and the life (Jn. 14:6); the true vine (Jn. 15:1).*

When the signs were misunderstood and when the direct statements were rejected, then Jesus resorted to the third phase, which was stating divine truths in parables.

With many similar parables Jesus spoke the word to them, as much as they could understand. He did not say anything to them without using a parable. But when he was alone with his own disciples, he explained everything. (Mark 4:33-34)

8. The Redemption of Sinners: a Revelation of the Power of God:

When I came to you, brothers, I did not come with eloquence or superior wisdom as I proclaimed to you the testimony about God. For I resolved to know nothing while I was with you except Jesus Christ and him crucified. I came to you in weakness and fear, and with much trembling. My message and my preaching were not with wise and persuasive words, but with a demonstration of the Spirit's power, so that your faith might not rest on men's wisdom, but on God's power. (1 Cor 2:1-5)

Grace and peace to you from God our Father and the Lord Jesus Christ, who gave himself for our sins to rescue us from the present evil age, according to the will of our God and Father, to whom be glory forever and ever. Amen. *(Gal 1:3-5)*

For it is by grace you have been saved, through faith — and this not from yourselves, it is the gift of God— not by works, so that no one can boast. For we are God's workmanship, created in Christ Jesus to do good works, which God prepared in advance for us to do. *(Eph 2:8-10)*

For the grace of God that brings salvation has appeared to all men. It teaches us to say "No" to ungodliness and worldly passions, and to live self-controlled, upright and godly lives in this present age, while we wait for the blessed hope — the glorious appearing of our great God and Savior, Jesus Christ, who gave himself for us to redeem us from all wickedness and to purify for himself a people that are his very own, eager to do what is good. *(Titus 2:11-14)*

When we speak of the power of God, we use the term as related to the Triune God. In the context of the present age, we are really talking about the authority and the power which the Father has given to the Son. This is the message of Daniel.

In my vision at night I looked, and there before me was one like a son of man [Christ], coming with the clouds of heaven. He approached the Ancient of Days [God] and was led into his presence. He was given authority, glory and sovereign power; all peoples, nations and men of every language worshiped him. His dominion is an everlasting dominion that will not pass away, and his kingdom is one that will never be destroyed. *(Dan 7:13-14)*

The Son of God has all authority and power, which has been given to Him by the Father. This is the truth and the witness of the Scriptures.

Further, this is true in both spiritual and in secular terms. In the secular world, the Scripture emphasized that "*there is no authority except that which God has established.*" Paul confirms this truth in Romans 13:1.

Everyone must submit himself to the governing authorities, for there is no authority except that which God has established. The authorities that exist have been established by God. (Rom 13:1)

Now to him who is able to do immeasurably more than all we ask or imagine, according to his power that is at work within us, to him be glory in the church and in Christ Jesus throughout all generations, forever and ever! Amen. (Eph 3:20-21)

9. The Witness of Individuals to the Power of God:

This section presents a brief description of the power of God in the lives of a few of the men/women who, by their faith, have witnessed to the power of God in different circumstances.

Those included are Esther, Shadrach, the apostles Peter/John, Paul, and conclude with Hebrew, chapter 11, the Hall of Fame of the people of faith.

The first is Queen Esther. This unusual book has great messages for Christians today; it speaks to the issues that we face and our willingness to accept the consequences for the actions we take. Esther knows of the potential genocide of the Jews, and Mordecai, her uncle, encouraged her to seek the king and plead for her people, the Jews.

Mordecai said to Esther: *"For if you [Esther] remain silent at this time, relief and deliverance for the Jews will arise from another place, but you and your father's family will perish. And who knows but that you have come to royal position for such a time as this?"*

Then Esther sent this reply to Mordecai: *"Go, gather together all the Jews who are in Susa, and fast for me. Do not eat or drink for three days, night or day. I and my maids will fast as you do. When this is done, I will go to the king, even though it is against the law. And if I perish, I perish." (Esther 4:14-16)*

Each one of us has a moment of decision when we must be confident in where God has placed us and what He calls us to do.

We are to stand firm, be faithful to God, and be willing to do what God would ask of us, whenever such situations arise.

The second example of the Presence of God is when Shadrach, Meshach, and Abednego, as commanded by King Nebuchadnezzar, were about to be thrown into the fiery furnace for refusing to bow down and worship the golden idol.

Shadrach, Meshach and Abednego replied to the king, "O Nebuchadnezzar, we do not need to defend ourselves before you in this matter. If we are thrown into the blazing furnace, the God we serve is able to save us from it, and he will rescue us from your hand, O king. But even if he does not, we want you to know, O king, that we will not serve your gods or worship the image of gold you have set up. (Dan 3:16-18)

The third example is that of Peter and John before the Sanhedrin, who had commanded them to refrain from speaking or teaching in the name of Jesus. The apostles spoke with boldness and confidence before the Sanhedrin, because they were convinced, regardless of the consequences, that they must obey God and not men. After their release, they rejoiced that they had been counted worthy to suffer for the sake of the gospel and the Christ whom they loved and served.

When they [Sanhedrin] saw the courage of Peter and John and realized that they were unschooled, ordinary men, they were astonished and they took note that these men had been with Jesus.... Then they called them in again and commanded them not to speak or teach at all in the name of Jesus. But Peter and John replied, "Judge for yourselves whether it is right in God's sight to obey you rather than God. For we cannot help speaking about what we have seen and heard." After further threats they let them go... On their release, Peter and John went back to their own people and reported all that the chief priests and elders had said to them. When they heard this, they raised their voices together in prayer to God. "Sovereign Lord," they said, "you made the heaven and the earth and the sea, and everything in them. You spoke by the Holy Spirit through the mouth of your servant, our father David: "Why do the nations rage and the peoples plot in vain? The kings of the earth take their stand and the rulers gather together against the Lord and against his Anointed One." (Acts 4:13, 18-26)

The final example is the apostle Paul.

Then Paul said: "I am a Jew, born in Tarsus of Cilicia, but brought up in this city. Under Gamaliel I was thoroughly trained in the law of our fathers and was just as zealous for God as any of you are today. I persecuted the followers of this Way to their death, arresting both men and women and throwing them into prison, as also the high priest and all the Council can testify. I even obtained letters from them to their brothers in Damascus, and went there to bring these people as prisoners to Jerusalem to be punished." (Acts 22:3-5)

Saul (Paul), the persecutor of the Jews, was called by Christ, out of his spiritual blindness to experience physical blindness, so that Paul could see the truth and serve the Living God. Paul met his Lord on that Damascus road: there the transformation of Paul was initiated.

Rather, as servants of God we commend ourselves in every way: in great endurance; in troubles, hardships and distresses; in beatings, imprisonments and riots; in hard work, sleepless nights and hunger; in purity, understanding, patience and kindness; in the Holy Spirit and in sincere love; in truthful speech and in the power of God; with weapons of righteousness in the right hand and in the left; through glory and dishonor, bad report and good report; genuine, yet regarded as impostors; known, yet regarded as unknown; dying, and yet we live on; beaten, and yet not killed; sorrowful, yet always rejoicing; poor, yet making many rich; having nothing, and yet possessing everything. (2 Cor 6:4-10)

In him you were also circumcised, in the putting off of the sinful nature, not with a circumcision done by the hands of men but with the circumcision done by Christ, having been buried with him in baptism and raised with him through your faith in the power of God, who raised him from the dead. (Col 2:11-12)

Peter replied, "Repent and be baptized, every one of you, in the name of Jesus Christ for the forgiveness of your sins. And you will receive the gift of the Holy Spirit. The promise is for you and your children and for all who are far off — for all whom the Lord our God will call." (Acts 2:38-39)

I have been crucified with Christ and I no longer live, but Christ lives in me. The life I live in the body, I live by faith in the Son of God, who loved me and gave himself for me. I do not set aside the grace of God, for if righteousness could be gained through the law, Christ died for nothing! (Gal 2:20-21)

In discussing the Gospel of Christ, Paul first directs our attention to the *power of God.*

We have seen the omnipotence of God as a witness to Himself.

We have seen Christ, the Son of God, as a witness to the power of God.

We have seen the witness of the written Word of God to His power.

We have seen the creation as a witness to His power.

We have seen the redemption of sinners as a witness to His power.

We have seen specific examples of faithful individuals as a witness to His power.

God is omnipotent; nothing can restrict the power of the Almighty God.

We now examine the salvation which God brought about through the gift of His Son, Jesus Christ.

Chapter 9

The gospel is the power of God for the salvation of everyone who believes (Rom 1:16)

Then Moses and the Israelites sang this song to the LORD: "I will sing to the LORD, for he is highly exalted. The horse and its rider he has hurled into the sea. The LORD is my strength and my song; he has become my salvation." (Exo 15:1-2)

But what does it say? "The word is near you; it is in your mouth and in your heart," that is, the word of faith we are proclaiming: That if you confess with your mouth, "Jesus is Lord," and believe in your heart that God raised him from the dead, you will be saved. (Rom 10:8-10)

And you also were included in Christ when you heard the word of truth, the gospel of your salvation. Having believed, you were marked in him with a seal, the promised Holy Spirit, who is a deposit guaranteeing our inheritance until the redemption of those who are God's possession — to the praise of his glory. (Eph 1:13-14)

For it is by grace you have been saved, through faith — and this not from yourselves, it is the [free] gift of God— not by works, so that no one can boast. For we are God's workmanship, created in Christ Jesus to do good works, which God prepared in advance for us to do. (Eph 2:8-10)

After this I heard what sounded like the roar of a great multitude in heaven shouting: "Hallelujah! Salvation and glory and power belong to our God, for true and just are his judgments." (Rev 19:1-2)

We now address the question of the *purpose of the gospel*, which is the *salvation of everyone who believes.*

The word, salvation, is found 80 times in the Old Testament and 42 times in the New Testament. Salvation is the redemption and transformation of sinners, reconciled to God, and equipped for every good work pleasing to God.

In every circumstance, the Holy Spirit leads the saints into all truth and thereby equips the saints with the power to proclaim the gospel and advance the Kingdom of God. The Holy Spirit equips the saints to be witnesses for Christ.

Before proceeding, consider the passages at the beginning of this chapter.

The first, Exodus 15:1-2, is the beginning of the song that Moses and the Israelites sang to God after being delivered from the hand of Pharaoh and crossing safely through the Red Sea.

The second, Romans 10:8-10, confirms that confession of Christ as Lord and belief in His resurrection are the basic statements of faith that leads to salvation.

The third, Ephesians 1:13-15, identifies the *gospel of your salvation* as the word of truth given to the redeemed by the Holy Spirit.

The fourth, Ephesians 2:8-10, states that the grace of God and our response in faith is the basis of salvation.

The fifth, Revelation 19:1-2, states that salvation is because God's judgments are true and just.

Salvation is the divine means by which man is equipped to attain to the highest good that God has prepared for him. Salvation has a dual meaning: it defines *deliverance from* all that restricts and prevents redemption and reconciliation with God, and being *transformed into* that in which mankind begins to approach the image of God (Gen 1:27).

However, the primary enemies of mankind are sin, death, and the devil. Sin is lawlessness and is the insidious illness which restricts redemption and a relationship with God. Death will be both physical and spiritual. Spiritual death is the state in which the individual is eternally separated from God. This is the second death (Rev 20:6). In all regards, spiritual death is the opposite of salvation.

Opposed to these enemies of mankind is the love of God which brings salvation and reconciliation with God. Opposed to union with God is spiritual death which means eternally separated from God and under the wrath of God.

The love of God is the foundation of our salvation.

The love of God is real; the wrath of God is real.

The love of God leads to salvation; the wrath of God leads to eternal condemnation and separation.

The Apostle Paul confirmed these truths.

Therefore, there is now no condemnation for those who are in Christ Jesus, because through Christ Jesus the law of the Spirit of life set me free from the law of sin and death. (Rom 8:1-2)

In the New Testament, salvation is regarded almost exclusively as freedom, release and pardon from the power and dominion of sin, death, and the devil. Jesus Christ is the Author of our salvation (Matt 1:21; Acts 4:12; Heb 2:10; 5:9), which is the free gift of God. However, it demands two acts: the first is that of *repentance from sin*; the second is *faith in Christ Jesus*.

Two companion passages (John 3:16-21; Ephesians 2:8-10) attest to this truth.

For God so loved the world that he gave his one and only Son, that whoever believes in him shall not perish but have eternal life. For God did not send his Son into the world to condemn the world, but to save the world through him. Whoever believes in him is not condemned, but whoever does not believe stands condemned already because he has not believed in the name of God's one and only Son. This is the verdict: Light has come into the world, but men loved darkness instead of light because their deeds were evil. Everyone who does evil hates the light, and will not come into the light for fear that his deeds will be exposed. But whoever lives by the truth comes into the light, so that it may be seen plainly that what he has done has been done through God. (John 3:16-21)

For it is by grace you have been saved, through faith — and this not from yourselves, it is the [free] gift of God— not by works, so that no one can boast. For we are God's workmanship, created in Christ Jesus to do good works, which God prepared in advance for us to do. (Eph 2:8-10)

In these passages from John and Ephesians, we see the basic conditions for salvation, in which the key words are *grace, faith,* and *saved.*

God's grace and our response in faith lead to salvation.

Grace is an overpowering word. Five letters which present and contain the primary essence of God's character and nature. God is love (I John 4:8), and His love has a dual character: it is grace and mercy. His grace is giving us what we do not deserve which is His love; His mercy is *not* giving us what we deserve, which is His wrath.

Faith is an equally significant word.

Now faith is the assurance of things hoped for, the conviction of things not seen. For by it the men of old received divine approval. By faith we understand that the world was created by the word of God, so that what is seen was made out of things which do not appear. (Heb 11:1-3 RSV)

Faith is the assurance and the conviction of the things of God. In addition, faith is the basis of divine approval. Further, the ultimate witness to faith is that the world was created by the word of God. Creation is by the *breath* of God.

Salvation proceeds from the love of God, is based upon the blood of Christ, is realized in forgiveness, pardon, redemption and reconciliation, and finally will be fully completed in the resurrection and glorification of all believers.

But the fate of man at judgment depends on what man is and does before judgment, so that the practical problem is salvation from the conditions that will bring the wrath of God in that judgment.

The need for salvation began in the Garden of Eden with the disobedience by Adam.

And the LORD God commanded the man, "You are free to eat from any tree in the garden; but you must not eat from the tree of the knowledge of good and evil, for when you eat of it you will surely die." (Gen 2:16-17)

Onto the scene came the serpent, the liar, the deceiver, the one who leads people away from God.

"You will not surely die," the serpent said to the woman. "For God knows that when you eat of it your eyes will be opened, and you will be like God, knowing good and evil." (Gen 3:4-5)

God knows both good and evil: more importantly, God knows the difference between good and evil. Even more important, God knows the consequences of doing good and doing evil.

To be like God requires the same wisdom and the same understanding. This subject of wisdom and understanding is one of the principal themes of the Book of Job (Job 38:36-37)

So Adam and Eve listened to the serpent, disobeyed God, sinned and separated themselves from God. They did what was forbidden and ate of the fruit of the tree of knowledge, because in doing so they *will be like God, knowing good and evil.*

They exchanged the truth, given by God, for the lies, given by the serpent. That unfortunate scenario had been played out daily, in every land by all people since that time.

Idolatry was the goal; disobedience was the act; separation from God was the result.

But there was a greater and more meaningful result; that was being forced out of the Garden and the loss of a divine relationship with God.

That disobedience led to their removal from the Garden, the initial *promised land*, and a foreshadowing of what will happen to all people and to all nations when idolatry is practiced and disobedience follows. This event in the first Garden will be repeated by the dispersion of the nation of Israel (722 BC) and the nation of Judah (586 BC). They too were removed from a different *promised land*, for continued disobedience.

So, the need for salvation dates back to man's removal from the Garden of Eden (Gen 3). After this Fall from grace, man's life was marked by strife and difficulty. Idolatry, violence, corruption, and greed dominated this world of darkness. Wickedness was the product of evil intent.

The LORD saw how great man's wickedness on the earth had become, and that every inclination of the thoughts of his heart was only evil all the time. The LORD was grieved that he had made man on the earth, and his heart was filled with pain. So the LORD said, "I will wipe mankind, whom I have created, from the face of the earth — men and animals, and creatures that move along the ground, and birds of the air — for I am grieved that I have made them." But Noah found favor in the eyes of the LORD. (Gen 6:5-8)

So God first dealt with sin by the destruction of all that was evil. A holy and just God cannot and will not abide with sin. There are consequences to sin; God's wrath is justly and righteously displayed in dealing with persistent sin.

When God destroyed almost all living creatures with the Flood, He also performed the first act of salvation by saving Noah and his family. The author of Hebrews captured the significance of the faith displayed by Noah; by his faith, Noah inherited a righteousness that resulted from his faith.

By faith Noah, when warned about things not yet seen, in holy fear [reverence] built an ark to save his family. By his faith he condemned the world and became heir of the righteousness that comes by faith. (Heb 11:7)

After the Flood, purification was short lived. In His eternal plan for redemption and reconciliation, God devised new ways to deal with sin and a disobedient people.

That brings us to the means of *salvation* as seen in the Old Testament.

With the Israelites in bondage in Egypt, God had a plan for their redemption. He selected a *deliverer* who would bring His people out of bondage and lead them to a land *flowing with milk and honey,* which was a foreshadowing of the eternal *promised land.*

Paradise Lost in the Garden will be regained in the New Heaven, the New Earth, and the New Jerusalem (Rev 21). With everything new, the people of God will know eternal fellowship with their Creator.

Much of Israel's worship of God was a remembrance of this experience that brought them from physical slavery in Egypt to freedom in the Promised Land (Ex 13:3-16). The saving power of God was demonstrated dramatically as God formed in the Israelites a holy nation of priestly servants of the Lord (Ex 19:4-6). The Exodus became a pattern of salvation by which God's future deeds of redemption and reconciliation would be understood.

But just as the Exodus symbolized their salvation, the Captivity of the Israelites in Babylon was a disastrous return to physical bondage because they were rebellious, stiff-necked, and disobedient.

Even in the Dispersion, the Israelites looked for a new and better Exodus (Isa 43:14-16) in which God would forgive their sins and restore their hearts (Jer 31:31-34). However, that never materialized.

This hope for a new Exodus merged with expectation of the rule of God (Ezek 36:22-38). Since God was Lord and had shown Himself to be righteous and faithful, He must one day overpower His enemies and perfect the life of His people. This hope is expressed through the concept of the *Day of the Lord* as described by the Old Testament prophets (e.g. Joel 2:1-11; Amos 9:11-15). But this hope also focused on the role of the Anointed King and the coming of the Messiah (Psa 2).

Even Israel's return from the Captivity, however, failed to fulfill all their hopes (e.g. Hag 2:3). So a new understanding arose: the full realization of God's purpose of salvation would involve the coming of a completely new age (Isa 65:17-25). This doctrine of salvation reached its fulfillment in the death of Christ on behalf of the world. Jesus' mission was to save the world from sin and the wrath of God (Matt 1:21; John 12:47; Rom 5:9). During His earthly ministry, salvation was offered through His Presence and the power of faith (Luke 19:9-10). Now, salvation is offered through Christ's death and resurrection (Mark 10:25).

However, disobedience and idolatry continued. Therefore, salvation was unavailable for such people.

To understand salvation, we begin by identifying the nature of mankind. The Scriptures emphasize: *all have sinned and fall short of the glory of God (Rom 3:23). There is none righteous, no, not one (Psa 3:9-18).* The whole world is guilty before God. This fact of universal human sin leads to the question in Job: *How then can a man be righteous before God? How can one born of woman be pure? (Job 25:4)*

The Old Testament answer is clear: *Do not bring your servant into judgment, for no one living is righteous before you [God]. (Ps 143:2)*

Paul gives the answer to the dilemma of sin by stating that we are *justified in Christ (Gal 2:17).* This expression, *in Christ,* means to be united to Christ, so as to exchange one's independence for the glory of union with Him. There are two ways in which this expression is used: *first,* it is used as the branch attached to the Vine [Christ] (John 15:5); *second,* it is used as being yoked with Christ (Matt 11:28-30).

I [Jesus] am the vine; you [my disciples] are the branches. If a man remains in me and I in him, he will bear much fruit; apart from me you can do nothing. (John 15:5)

Come to me [Christ], all you who are weary and burdened, and I will give you rest. Take my yoke upon you and learn from me, for I am gentle and humble in heart, and you will find rest for your souls. For my yoke is easy and my burden is light. (Matt 11:28-30)

In the passage from Matthew, Christ is not talking about rest from physical labor: no, Christ said that *I will give you rest for your soul.* Christ is talking about a spiritual rest. In addition, this is the only passage in which Christ described Himself, as *gentle and humble in heart.*

The salvation that comes through Christ may be described in three tenses: past, present, and future. When a person believes in Christ, he *is saved* (Acts 16:31). But we are also in the process of *being saved* from the power of sin and death (Rom 8:13; Phil 2:12). Finally, we *shall be saved* from the very presence of sin (Rom 13:11; Titus 2:12-13). God releases into our lives today the power of Christ's resurrection (Rom 6:4) and allows us a foretaste of our future life as His children (2 Cor 1:22; Eph 1:14). Our experience of salvation will be complete when Christ returns (Heb 9:28) and the kingdom of God is fully revealed (Matt 13:41-43).

The term, salvation, has four components or progressions: *justification,* followed by *sanctification,* then *edification, and* finally *glorification.*

Important companions to salvation are the two Christ-ordained sacraments of baptism and the Eucharist: these two sacraments will be discussed later in this chapter.

First, Justification:

The ultimate truth regarding justification is that which Paul identifies in 2 Corinthians 5:21. *God made him who had no sin to be sin for us, so that in him we might become the righteousness of God. (2 Cor 5:21)* This is one of the most remarkable passages in Scripture. The situation is this: we are sinners; Christ is the righteousness of God. On the Cross, Christ took on our sins; on the Cross, the righteousness of Christ was *transferred* to us. On the Cross, Christ became sin; at the Cross, we became righteous before God.

Justification means that sins have been confessed and repentance is sought. As a result, the sins are forgiven, the individual is pardoned, and the individual is declared innocent and set free. Christ's one act of righteousness brought justification for all men. Justification results in the sinner becoming righteous. In addition, repentance has the character of death and resurrection; we are dead in sin and made alive in Christ.

We die to the old self; we are raised to a new creation in Jesus, the Christ.

Repentance involves two decisions and two acts; first, we *turn away* from the wickedness of our former life; second, we *turn to* the new life in Christ. We turn away; we turn to. Both acts must occur.

He [Christ] was delivered over to death for our sins and was raised to life for our justification. (Rom 4:25)

Consequently, just as the result of one trespass was condemnation for all men, so also the result of one act of righteousness was justification that brings life for all men. For just as through the disobedience of the one man the many were made sinners, so also through the obedience of the one man the many will be made righteous. (Rom 5:18-19)

Justification is God's declaration that His holy and just demands have been fulfilled through the righteousness of His Son. The basis for justification is the death of Christ. Paul tells us that *God was in Christ reconciling the world to Himself, not imputing their trespasses to them (2 Cor 5:19)*. This reconciliation covers all sin: *For by one offering He has perfected forever those who are being sanctified (Heb 10:14)*.

Justification is the work of Christ, accomplished through His blood (Rom 5:9) and made available through His resurrection (Rom 4:25).

Justification is an unbelievable supernatural event. When God justifies, He charges the sin of man to Christ and credits the righteousness of Christ to the believer (2 Cor 5:21). Thus, *through one Man's righteous act, the free gift came to all men, resulting in justification of life (Rom 5:18). Because this righteousness is the righteousness of God which is apart from the law (Rom 3:21).* It is thorough and complete: a believer is *justified from all things* (Acts 13:39). God is *just* because His standard of perfect righteousness has been fulfilled in Christ, who is the *Justifier*, because He freely gave His righteousness to the repentant believer (Rom 3:26; 5:16).

I repeat; justification is a remarkable transformation. Christ assumes our sin; we receive His righteousness. Remarkable!

Although the Lord Jesus has paid the price for our justification, it is through faith that He is received and His righteousness is experienced and enjoyed (Rom 3:25-30).

What does the Scripture say? "Abraham believed God, and it was credited to him as righteousness." (Rom 4:3)

In this passage, belief in God is synonymous with faith in God. Faith is also the foundation of righteousness. As our faith increases, our righteousness increases.

Faith is considered, not as the work of *man* (Rom 4:5), but as the work and gift of God (John 6:28-29; Phil 1:29).

Not only is Christ's righteousness accounted to the believer, but Christ also dwells in the believer through the Holy Spirit (Rom 8:10), creating works of faith (Eph 2:10). Certainly God's works will be declared righteous (Isa 26:12). If this is true, then the order of events in justification is grace, faith, and works; or, in other words, by grace, through faith, resulting in works (Eph 2:8-10).

Justification is God's work; our response in faith is our work.

We continually remember before our God and Father your work produced by faith, your labor prompted by love, and your endurance inspired by hope in our Lord Jesus Christ. (1 Thess 1:3)

Consider it pure joy, my brothers, whenever you face trials of many kinds, because you know that the testing of your faith develops perseverance. Perseverance must finish its work so that you may be mature and complete, not lacking anything. (James 1:2-5)

Show me your faith without deeds, and I will show you my faith by what I do. (James 2:18)

Justification has many positive results: *first,* we are *saved from. Having now been justified...we shall be saved from wrath (Rom 5:9). Second,* we are *saved to: Whom He justified, these He also glorified (Rom 8:30).* Justification is the first step toward final glorification.

Other positive benefits of justification are *peace with God (Rom 5:1),* and *access to God's grace* (Rom 5:2), the redemption of our bodies (Rom 8:23) and an eternal inheritance (Rom 8:17; 1 Peter 1:4).

However, the companion to justification is sanctification.

Second, Sanctification:

Sanctification is being set apart, and make holy to love and serve the will and the purpose of God. It is the process of God's grace by which the believer is separated from sin and is committed to God.

It is what Paul called an *undivided devotion (I Cor 7:35).* Accomplished by the Word of God (John 17:7) and the Holy Spirit (Rom 8:3-4), sanctification results in holiness and purification from the power of sin.

Sanctification is spiritual separation from the world and being set apart for God's service. Our example is that Jesus was *sanctified and sent into the world (John 10:36).* In the same way, we are to be sanctified and sent into the world. We are sent into the world but we are to be separated from the things of the world.

Christians are to be in the world, bringing light to the darkness (John 1:3); we are to be in the world but not of the world. We are to be the light of the world, so that those living in darkness will see the light and turn to Christ for forgiveness, pardon, redemption, and reconciliation with God.

We are to seek the things above, not the things of this world.

Since, then, you have been raised with Christ, set your hearts on things above, where Christ is seated at the right hand of God. Set your minds on things above, not on earthly things. For you died, and your life is now hidden with Christ in God. When Christ, who is your life, appears, then you also will appear with him in glory. (Col 3:1-4)

In the same way, count yourselves dead to sin but alive to God in Christ Jesus. (Rom 6:11)

Sanctification is based on the sacrificial death of Christ and leads to the purification of believers.

In his epistles, the Apostle Paul noted that God has *chosen* and *reconciled* us to Himself in Christ for the purpose of sanctification (Eph 1:4; 5:25-27; Titus 2:14).

Sanctification is God's work. We are sanctified by God the Father (Jude), God the Son (Heb 2:11), and God the Holy Spirit (2 Thess 2:13; 1 Peter 1:2). Perfect holiness is God's vision (1 Thess 4:7) and purpose. As Paul prayed: *Now may the God of peace Himself sanctify you completely (1 Thess 5:23).*

Sanctification is also our work. The Bible states that believers have a responsibility in sanctification. We are commanded to *be holy* (Lev 11:44; 1 Peter 1:15-16); to *be perfect* (Matt 5:48); and to *present your members as slaves of righteousness for holiness* (Rom 6:19). Writing to the church of the Thessalonians, Paul made a strong plea for purity: *This is the will of God, your sanctification: that you should abstain from sexual immorality; that each of you should know how to possess his own vessel in sanctification and honor, not in passion of lust, like the Gentiles who do not know God. (1 Thess 4:3-5)*

These commands require a sincere effort on our part. We must believe in Jesus, since we are *sanctified by faith in Him (Acts 26:18).* Through the Holy Spirit, we must also *put to death the evil deeds of the body (Rom 8:13).* Paul itemized the many *works of the flesh* from which we must separate ourselves (Gal 5:19-21). Finally, we must walk in the Spirit in order to display the fruit of the Spirit (Gal 5:22-24).

We now address, edification, the third stage of salvation.

Third, Edification:

Edification is being led by the Spirit into all truth (John 16:13) and being raised up into maturity in Christ.

Him [Christ] we proclaim, warning every man and teaching every man in all wisdom, that we may present every man mature in Christ. For this I toil, striving with all the energy which he mightily inspires within me. (Col 1:28-29 RSV)

Then Jesus came to them and said, "All authority in heaven and on earth has been given to me. Therefore go and make disciples of all nations, baptizing them in the name of the Father and of the Son and of the Holy Spirit, and teaching them to obey everything I have commanded you. And surely I am with you always, to the very end of the age." (Matt 28:18-20)

In Galatians, Paul spoke of being crucified with Christ, so that Christ would live in him.

For through the law I died to the law so that I might live for God. I have been crucified with Christ and I no longer live, but Christ lives in me. The life I live in the body, I live by faith in the Son of God, who loved me and gave himself for me. (Gal 2:19-20)

These examples describe how we will be edified: *first*, faith (Gal 2:15-16); *second*, Christ formed in you (Gal 4:19); *third*, we are to live by the Spirit (Gal 5:16); *fourth*, we will become a new creation (Gal 5:16)

Therefore, if anyone is in Christ, he is a new creation; the old has gone, the new has come! (2 Cor 5:17)

To be edified and grow in maturity requires the following: *first*, the study and hearing of God's Word; *second*, prayer; *third*, meditation; and *fourth*, being a faithful witness to Jesus Christ and to His resurrection. We are called to edify or *build up one another* (1 Thess 5:11) by the example of love.

Let us therefore make every effort to do what leads to peace and to mutual edification. (Rom 14:19)

We now move to glorification, the final stage in the process of salvation.

Fourth, Glorification:

Glorification is that final stage when we shall have glorified bodies, spending eternity with the God and the Father of all. The salvation depicted here is the result of redemption, reconciliation, the resurrection of the believer, and the promise of eternal life.

The question is: what will our glorified bodies resemble? The Bible states that they will not resemble anything with which we are familiar. Instead, the closest we might come is to understand what Scripture tells us about the resurrected body of Christ. After His resurrection, His body was physical, but it was not limited by any physical restraints. Somehow, He was recognized. He could be touched; He was visible; He could pass through walls. He was physical without any physical limitations.

So, salvation is the sequential actions of justification, sanctification, edification, and glorification.

In every case, grace is the foundation of salvation.

However, we have a distinct role to play, and the apostle Paul defined that role.

For it is by grace you have been saved, through faith — and this not from yourselves, it is the [free] gift of God— not by works, so that no one can boast. For we are God's workmanship, created in Christ Jesus to do good works, which God prepared in advance for us to do. (Eph 2:8-10)

In this passage, God gives us His grace; we respond in faith; the result is salvation.

It is the free gift of God; salvation is not by our works; it is by our faith.

Paul explained the result of our salvation. It is this: we are God's workmanship, created in Christ Jesus to do good works, which God prepared in advance for us to do. Tomorrow is already planned by God; we just have to show up for work.

When we receive Christ and believe in His name (John 1:12), we receive the power, the liberty, and the freedom to be born of the Spirit which identifies us as a child of God.

We receive justification as a gift; we are sanctified by God; we are edified by the Holy Spirit; we are glorified by God. It is all through Him and by Him.

And those he [God] predestined, he also called; those he called, he also justified; those he justified, he also glorified. (Rom 8:30)

For you know that it was not with perishable things such as silver or gold that you were redeemed from the empty way of life handed down to you from your forefathers, but with the precious blood of Christ, a lamb without blemish or defect. He [Christ] was chosen before the creation of the world, but was revealed in these last times for your sake. Through him [Christ] you believe in God, who raised him from the dead and glorified him, and so your faith and hope are in God. (1 Peter 1:18-21)

It is by faith, that we are acceptable to God. It is by faith that we believe in God. It is through Christ that we have come to believe in God.

We are to have the mind of Christ.

Have this mind among yourselves, which is yours in Christ Jesus, (Phil 2:5 RSV)

We are to imitate Christ; imitate those who have faith and patience.

We do not want you to become lazy, but to imitate those who through faith and patience inherit what has been promised. (Heb 6:12)

In our lives, we are to seek the things of God, which will lead to our noblest thoughts and actions.

Finally, brothers, whatever is true, whatever is noble, whatever is right, whatever is pure, whatever is lovely, whatever is admirable — if anything is excellent or praiseworthy — think about such things. Whatever you have learned or received or heard from me, or seen in me — put it into practice. And the God of peace will be with you. (Phil 4:8-9)

Since, then, you have been raised with Christ, set your hearts on things above, where Christ is seated at the right hand of God. Set your minds on things above, not on earthly things. For you died, and your life is now hidden with Christ in God. When Christ, who is your life, appears, then you also will appear with him in glory. (Col 3:1-4)

But we have to raise this question. What is our attitude by which we approach the Presence of God? What is our attitude towards God and the things of God? What is our attitude.....?

Charles Swindoll has this to say about our attitude.

"The longer I live, the more I realize the impact of attitude on life. Attitude to me is more important than facts. It is more important than the past, than education, than money, than circumstances, than failures, than successes, than what other people think or say or do. It is more important than appearance, giftedness, or skill. It will make or break a company...a church...a home. The remarkable thing is we will embrace it for that day. We cannot change our past...we cannot change the fact that people will act in a certain way. We cannot change the inevitable. The only thing we can do is play on the one string we have, and that is our attitude...I am convinced that life is 10% what happens to me and 90% how I react to it. And so it is with you...we are in charge of our attitudes."

Recall the experience of Job with God. Job thought that he knew God, because *This man [Job] was blameless and upright; he feared [reverenced] God and shunned evil. (Job 1:1)* However, as the Book of Job unfolds, it becomes clear that Job had much to learn about the ways and the will of God. Towards the end of the Book, we see this exchange between God and Job.

Where were you [Job] when I [God] laid the earth's foundation? Tell me, if you understand. Who marked off its dimensions? Surely you know! (Job 38:4-5)

Then Job replied to the LORD: "I know that you can do all things; no plan of yours can be thwarted. [You asked,] 'Who is this that obscures my counsel without knowledge?' Surely I spoke of things I did not understand, things too wonderful for me to know. (Job 42:1-3)

In like manner, King David spoke of how he was overwhelmed by the divine knowledge and wisdom of God. *You [God] hem me in — behind and before; you have laid your hand upon me. Such knowledge is too wonderful for me, too lofty for me to attain......Search me, O God, and know my heart; test me and know my anxious thoughts. See if there is any offensive way in me, and lead me in the way everlasting. (Ps 139:5-6)*

The apostle Paul said that he looked though a glass darkly, but one day, face to face, he would know all things. That is equally true for us. We don't know all things; we don't need to know all things. That is a hard lesson for Christians to learn.

Now we see but a poor reflection as in a mirror; then we shall see face to face. Now I know in part; then I shall know fully, even as I am fully known. (1 Cor 13:12)

Job, King David, Paul—all spoke of the great wisdom and knowledge of God. A wisdom and knowledge that is too wonderful, too lofty, which we can only get a glimpse of. Like them, we tend to think of things too wonderful for us.

Instead we need to approach any understanding of God with the greatest of humility. We cannot prove all things; but, praise God, we don't need to prove all things. And the beauty of it is that faith takes hold where human knowledge ceases.

And he said to man, "The fear [reverence] of the Lord — that is wisdom, and to shun evil is understanding." (Job 28:28)

The fear [reverence] of the LORD is the beginning of wisdom, and knowledge of the Holy One is understanding. (Prov 9:10)

God's word tells us that the fear of the Lord, our holy reverence for God, is the beginning of wisdom. In addition, knowledge and understanding that come from two sources: first, because we shun evil; second, because we have the knowledge of God, the Holy One.

Are there some things that are beyond human reason? Without a doubt!

Do we believe that our knowledge is sufficient for our purposes? No way!

Do we believe that which we cannot prove? Absolutely!

When our sins were taken by Christ, there was a great darkness over all the earth; this occurred during His crucifixion. Darkness symbolizes the presence of sin.

It was now about the sixth hour, and darkness came over the whole land until the ninth hour, for the sun stopped shining. And the curtain of the temple was torn in two. Jesus called out with a loud voice, "Father, into your hands I commit my spirit." When he had said this, he breathed his last. (Luke 23:44-46)

This total darkness represented the sin of all mankind, for no eye should see the enormity of the sins of the world that filled the sinless body of the Son of God.

The divine dilemma was the manner in which a holy God would deal with sin. For sin by its very nature represents disobedience and disobedience is the act that separates sinful man from a holy God. God cannot abide sin. There are consequences to sin; and the undeniable truth is that no individual nor any nation nor any people nor any culture is immune from the wrath of God against sin.

Sin is lawlessness: it is the result of disobedience to the commandments and overall Will of God. Sin is therefore dangerous not only because it breaks God's laws; but more importantly, sin breaks a relationship—and that relationship is with a holy God, who is the Creator, Sustainer, and Provider of all that is essential for life.

So the question is: how could a holy God remain true to Himself and His holy nature—and accept and love sinners who had corrupted His divine plan for His creation?

Further: how does God restore unity with His created order and develop a fellowship that He had always desired?

God needed a solution to reconcile evil and sinful mankind with their Maker.

How does God redeem and reconcile fallen mankind to a divine relationship with Him? God's answer is the Cross of Christ.

To complete our discussion on salvation, it is necessary to consider the Passover, the Exodus, the Eucharist, and the Cross.

In many ways, the gospel is a spiritual reenactment of both the Passover and the Exodus, which foreshadow the Eucharist and the Cross.

The Passover foreshadows the Eucharist; the Exodus foreshadows the Cross. This relationship between the Exodus and the Cross has already been discussed in Chapter 4.

However, as essential to our understanding of salvation, let us now consider the relationship of the Passover and the companion feast, the Feast of Unleavened Bread, as they foreshadow the Christian Eucharist (The Lord's Supper; Holy Communion), which Christ initiated and which He commanded us to celebrate in remembrance of Him.

To begin with, let us first consider the Passover and the Feast of Unleavened Bread. The Passover celebrated the *protection* of the people of God from the angels of death; the Feast of Unleavened Bread celebrated the *provision* of God for His people.

The Passover referred to the sacrifice of a lamb in Egypt when the people of Israel were slaves. The Hebrews smeared the blood of the paschal lamb on their doorposts as protection against the angels of death which God had sent to kill the firstborn male of each Egyptian family, as a warning to Pharaoh to let His people go. Unleavened bread was used in the celebration because this showed that the people had no time to put leaven in their bread as they ate their final meal as slaves in Egypt.

Regulations were given by God concerning the observance of Passover, among which was the place where it was to be observed, as well as the regulation that none of the bones of the lamb should be broken. Passover was to be observed *"in the place which the Lord your God will choose."* This statement was considered to mean the sanctuary of the tabernacle or the Temple in Jerusalem.

The LORD said to Moses and Aaron, "These are the regulations for the Passover: No foreigner is to eat of it. Any slave you have bought may eat of it after you have circumcised him, but a temporary resident and a hired worker may not eat of it. It must be eaten inside one house; take none of the meat outside the house. Do not break any of the bones. The whole community of Israel must celebrate it." (Ex 12:43-47)

In like manner, Jesus is the paschal lamb, sent by God, to die for the sins of the world. *The next day John saw Jesus coming toward him and said, "Look, the Lamb of God, who takes away the sin of the world! (John 1:29)*

As the crucified Savior, the regulation that none of the bones of the lamb were to be broken was particularly significant. At His crucifixion, none of the bones of Jesus were broken, conforming to the regulations of the Passover, first expressed in Exodus 12:43-47. The Scriptures attest to this truth.

But when they [the soldiers] came to Jesus and found that he was already dead, they did not break his legs. (John 19:33)

When Jesus met with His disciples in that upper room to celebrate the Passover, He made two monumental changes in the Passover service.

First, He took the bread and said: this is my body *given for you.* He did not say: *broken for you.* Such a statement, used in many Eucharist services, is inappropriate. Second, He took the cup of wine and said: this is my blood, shed for you to ratify the new covenant (Jeremiah 31:31-34) for the forgiveness of sins.

And he took bread, gave thanks and broke it, and gave it to them, saying, "This is my body given for you; do this in remembrance of me." In the same way, after the supper he took the cup, saying, "This cup is the new covenant [for the forgiveness of sins] in my blood, which is poured out for you. (Luke 22:19-20)

And so salvation is based on the grace of God with our response in faith. Salvation is though faith alone in Christ alone. The Eucharist commemorates the death of Christ for the forgiveness of sins and for reconciliation with God.

Chapter 10

The gospel is the power of God for the salvation of **everyone who believes** (Rom 1:16)

He [Christ] came to that which was his own, but his own did not receive him. Yet to all who received him, to those who believed in his name, he gave the right to become children of God— children born not of natural descent, nor of human decision or a husband's will, but born of God. (John 1:11-13)

What does the Scripture say? "Abraham believed God, and it was credited to him as righteousness." (Rom 4:3)

Understand, then, that those who believe are children of Abraham. The Scripture foresaw that God would justify the Gentiles by faith, and announced the gospel in advance to Abraham: "All nations will be blessed through you." So those who have faith are blessed along with Abraham, the man of faith. (Gal 3:7-9)

For we also have had the gospel preached to us, just as they did; but the message they heard was of no value to them, because those who heard did not combine it with faith. Now we who have believed enter that rest, just as God has said, "So I declared on oath in my anger, 'They shall never enter my rest.'" (Heb 4:2-3)

There are two important thoughts in this chapter: the first is: the gospel is for *everyone*. The second is: salvation is for *everyone who believes*.

However, consider the passages at the beginning of this chapter.

The first, John 1:11-13, states that the children of God are those who have *received* the Lord Jesus and *believed* in His name. Because of that dual affirmation, those who *believe* will be born of the Spirit and be children of God.

The second, Romans 4:3, states that Abraham's faith in God was the foundation of his righteousness. Faith leads to righteousness.

The third, Galatians 3:7-9, contains five statements: *first,* the true children of Abraham are those who believe as Abraham believed; *second*, the Scriptures reaffirm that God would justify the Gentiles by faith; *third,* God announced the gospel initially through Abraham; *fourth,* all nations will be blessed though Abraham and his offspring; *fifth,* all who have faith will be blessed along with Abraham, the man of faith. It is important to recognize that the blessing to the nations will come through Abraham and his offspring, who is Jesus Christ.

The fourth, Hebrew 4:2-3, states that the message of salvation can be heard; but, unless we respond in faith, the message has *no value* to us.

What is the significance of the phrase, *everyone who believes?* This phrase demands our attention.

So, first, we will discuss this designation of *everyone*.

Second, the word, *believes,* is a vitally important and all-encompassing word: it has meaning for those who repent, those of hope, those of faith, and those of righteousness.

First, everyone

On the negative side, we see that not everyone will be saved through the power of God: we understand that not everyone will know the love of God. However, we do know that everyone will have eternal life (Dan 12:1-2).

At that time Michael, the great prince who protects your people, will arise. There will be a time of distress such as has not happened from the beginning of nations until then. But at that time your people — everyone whose name is found written in the book — will be delivered. Multitudes who sleep in the dust of the earth will awake: some to everlasting life, others to shame and everlasting contempt. (Dan 12:1-2)

This passage from Daniel confirms the truth of a general resurrection with two alternatives: first, some to everlasting life; second, others to shame and everlasting contempt.

We will see that the love of God, salvation, and eternal life are given to *everyone who believes. The key is to believe.*

For those who do not believe, they will face the consequences of their sin and continued rebellion against God. Instead of love, they will experience the wrath of God.

The wrath of God is being revealed from heaven against all the godlessness and wickedness of men who suppress the truth by their wickedness, since what may be known about God is plain to them, because God has made it plain to them. For since the creation of the world God's invisible qualities — his eternal power and divine nature — have been clearly seen, being understood from what has been made, so that men are without excuse. (Rom 1:18-20)

The love of God brings blessings, peace, and rewards; the wrath of God brings warnings, severe consequences, and punishment.

The message of salvation is for everyone: however, the message may be ignored or rejected by many.

Recall that God told Abraham: *all nations on earth will be blessed through you. (Gen 18:18)*

Notice throughout that the message is for *all nations, for everyone.*

The gospel is for everyone. The question is: will everyone accept the gospel?

The record is clear; not everyone will accept the gospel of Christ.

Many reject the gospel because it demands too much; it requires surrender and obedience and love.

However, consider the glory that is found in the meaning of *everyone* who believes.

And everyone who calls on the name of the LORD will be saved; (Joel 2:32)

For everyone who asks receives; he who seeks finds; and to him who knocks, the door will be opened. (Matt 7:8)

So I say to you: Ask and it will be given to you; seek and you will find; knock and the door will be opened to you. For everyone *who asks receives; he who seeks finds; and to him who knocks, the door will be opened. (Luke 11:9-10)*

For everyone who exalts himself will be humbled, and he who humbles himself will be exalted. (Luke 4:11)

Just as Moses lifted up the snake in the desert, so the Son of Man must be lifted up, that everyone who believes in him may have eternal life. (John 3:14-15)

Christ is the end of the law so that there may be righteousness for everyone who believes. (Rom 10:4)

We proclaim him, admonishing and teaching everyone with all wisdom, so that we may present everyone perfect in Christ. To this end I labor, struggling with all his energy, which so powerfully works in me. (Col 1:28-29)

The Lord is not slow in keeping his promise, as some understand slowness. He is patient with you, not wanting anyone to perish, but everyone to come to repentance. (2 Peter 3:8-9)

Dear friends, let us love one another, for love comes from God. Everyone who loves has been born of God and knows God. Whoever does not love does not know God, because God is love. This is how God showed his love among us: He sent his one and only Son into the world that we might live through him. This is love: not that we loved God, but that he loved us and sent his Son as an atoning sacrifice for our sins. Dear friends, since God so loved us, we also ought to love one another.

No one has ever seen God; but if we love one another, God lives in us and his love is made complete in us. (1 John 4:7-12)

In all those passages, look at the fruit that is available for *everyone*.

Second, believe:

To believe is to accept a truth and to remain steadfast in conviction regarding that truth. It means to accept God's promises, but it also means to obey God's commandments.

And what does believing require? It requires Christian faith in Christian hope. Believing leads to righteousness; believing leads to repentance.

To believe is critically important to the Christian life here and now—and as the foundation of eternity.

Believing is seen in at least four areas: in hope, in faith, in righteousness, and in repentance. Their combined understanding will equip us to understand those *who believe*.

Christian hope is what God offers, as distinguished from faith, which is our response to hope.

Hope distinguishes Christians from unbelievers who have no hope (Eph 2:12; I Thess 4:13). Indeed, the hope of God resides in each Christian (I Pet 3:15; I John 3:3). In contrast to Old Testament hope, the Christian hope is superior (Heb 7:19). Christian hope comes from God (Rom 15:13); it is the result of His election (Eph 1:18, 4:4), His grace (2 Thess 2:16), His Word (Rom 15:4) and His gospel (Col 1:23). Hope is directed from God and towards God (Acts 24:15; I Pet 1:21) and Christ (I Thess 1:3; 1 Tim 1:1). Its appropriate objects are salvation (I Thess 5:6), righteousness (Gal 5:5), the glory of God (Rom 5:2; Col 1:27), the return of Christ (Titus 2:13), the resurrection from the dead (Acts 23:6, 26:6-7) and eternal life (Titus 1:2, 3:7)

Christians are people of hope. However, what are our greatest hopes?

I submit: there are at least two. The answer: first, *Christ in you, the hope of glory (Col 1:27)*; second, the certainty, the hope of eternal life.

Eternal life is our redeemed existence in Jesus Christ which is granted by God to all believers. Eternal life refers to the quality or character of our new existence in Christ. The phrase, everlasting life, is found in the Old Testament only once (Dan 12:2). But the idea of eternal life is implied by the prophets in their pictures of the glorious future promised to God's people.

Everyone will be resurrected; everyone will face the Final Judgment; everyone will have eternal life.

The question is: where will it be spent? Will it be spent in eternity with God: or will it be spent in shame and everlasting contempt?

The phrase, eternal life, appears most often in the Gospel of John and the Epistle of 1 John. John emphasized eternal life as the present possession of the Christian (John 3:36; 5:24; 1 John 5:13). John declared that the Christian believer has already begun to experience the blessings of the future even before their fullest expression: *And this is eternal life, that they may know You, the only true God, and Jesus Christ whom You have sent. (John 17:3).*

Eternal life is a priceless treasure, the gift of God. It is not to be confused with endless existence which all possess, the saved as well as the unsaved.

Eternal life can be viewed as a quantity or a quality. However, it is not the quantity of existence; it is the spiritual quality of divine existence in eternity with God.

Christ said, *I came that they might have life, and might have it abundantly (John 10:10).* This eternal life is nothing less than *Christ in you, the hope of glory (Col 1:27).* It is like a birth from above (John 3:3; 1:13) and is dependent upon receiving Christ as Savior. *He who has the Son has the life; he who does not have the Son of God does not have the life (1 John 5:12).*

Eternal life must not be confused with natural life. The natural life is subject to physical death and is derived by human generation.

Spiritual life has a beginning but no ending. Those possessing only natural life will be separated eternally from God in the lake of fire: those possessing eternal life will be united in fellowship with God for all eternity. Thus, separation from God is eternal death; union with God is eternal life.

The *Christian hope* is centered on eternal life with God the Father.

Next, consider Christian faith as a measure of belief.

Christian faith is defined in Hebrews 11:1. *Now faith is the assurance of things hoped for, the conviction of things not seen. (RSV)*

We have talked about hope and faith: but what is the relation between faith and hope?

The Scriptures present this truth: *hope* is that which God offers; *faith* is our assurance in what God offers.

In a scriptural sense, faith represents three basic ideas. The *first* is personal confidence in God; *second,* an understanding of revealed truth through the Spirit (Luke 18:8; 1 Cor 16:13; 2 Cor 13:5; Col 1:23; 2:7; Titus 1:13; Jude 3); *third,* Christ as the object of faith (Rom 3:22-25).

In addition, confidence in God is expressed in three types of faith: saving faith, sanctifying faith, and serving faith.

Saving faith is confidence in God's promises and provisions in Christ for the salvation of sinners. It leads to trust solely in the Person and work of Jesus Christ (John 3:16; 5:24; Eph 2:8-10). Such faith gives the believer the confidence of a life lived *in Christ* (Rom 8:1; Eph 1:3).

Sanctifying faith expresses trust in our life *in Christ* (Rom 6:1-10). All believers have been sanctified (1 Cor 1:2), are *saints of God,* and, by faith, are to live a life glorifying to God (Eph 4:1; Col 3:1-4). All believers who have exercised *saving faith* in Christ are what they are *in Him.*

Serving faith acts upon the spiritual gifts and has confidence in our divine election for service. This faith is a personal, individual matter. This is the call that God puts on our hearts.

The gift is for everyone; the basis of the gift is our belief.

However, *righteousness* is equally a measure of belief.

And the scripture was fulfilled that says, "Abraham believed God, and it was credited to him as righteousness," and he was called God's friend. (James 2:23-24)

Both Paul and James are quoting from Genesis 15:6, in which God's covenant with Abram contained this promise that God would give Abram a son and that all the nations would be blessed through him. *Abram believed the LORD, and he [God] credited it to him [Abram] as righteousness. (Gen 15:6)*

To *believe* means to have total trust in God, for all things and in all circumstances, and under all conditions. To those who believe, righteousness is one of the results.

The more we trust God, the greater becomes our righteousness.

We have to learn that God is the source of all; *that all things are his, no gifts have we to offer thee.* That is the simple, but complete, understanding that we must have.

For from him and through him and to him are all things. To him be the glory forever! Amen (Rom 11:36)

So belief is a foundation for righteousness.

But belief also is the basis of *repentance*.

Repentance requires two distinct but interrelated acts. It is first a *turning away* from sin, disobedience, and rebellion; second, it is a *turning to* God (Matt 9:13; Luke 5:32). Both steps must occur.

Confession of sins, repentance, and confession of Christ are the foundation of baptism, in which we die to the old and rise anew. Baptism is death and resurrection. The *old person* goes under the water and spiritually dies; the *new person* rises out of the water with a new perspective and a new relationship with God.

In much the same way, baptism represents a change of allegiance. We die to the old allegiance which ruled our lives; we rise up out of the water, claiming a new allegiance to a new King and a new way of life.

Repentance is necessary because of the sin in our lives. And sin represents more than just breaking a law; in our sins, we have broken a relationship, and that relationship was with God. Sin separates us from God: sin is spiritual death. Satan seeks no more than to separate you from God.

Therefore the purpose of repentance is to restore the broken relationship with God.

I would like to close with a quote from David Wilkerson: *God is Faithful: A Daily Invitation into the Father Heart of God.*

To believe when all means fail is exceedingly pleasing to God and is most acceptable. Jesus said to Thomas, "you have believed because you have seen, but blessed are those that do believe and have not seen" (john 20:29)

Blessed are those who believed when there is no evidence of an answer to prayer, who trust beyond hope when all means have failed.

Someone had come to the place of hopelessness, the end of hope, the end of all means. A loved one is facing death, and doctors give no hope. Death seems inevitable. Hope is gone. The miracle prayed for is not happening.

This is when Satan's hordes come to attack your mind with fear, anger, overwhelming questions: "Where is your God now? You prayed until you had no tears left. You fasted. You stood on promises. You trusted."

Blasphemous thoughts will be injected into your mind: "Prayer failed. Faith failed. Don't quit on God—just don't trust him anymore. It doesn't pay!"

To those going through the valley and shadow of death, hear this word; weeping will last through some dark, awful nights—and in that darkness you will soon hear the Father whisper, "I am with you. I cannot tell you why right now, but one day it will all make sense. You will see it was all part of my plan. It was no accident. It was no failure on your part. Hold fast. Let me embrace you in your hour of pain."

Beloved, God has never failed to act but in goodness and love. When all means fail, His love prevails. Hold fast to your faith. Stand fast in His word.

There is no other hope in this world.

We have completed now the definition of the gospel of Christ. *It is the power of God for the salvation of everyone who believes.*

We now turn to the gospel message: *the righteous will live by faith. (Habakkuk 2:4; Romans 1:17)*

Chapter 11

The Gospel Message

The **righteous** will live by faith (Rom 1:17)

For it is not those who hear the law who are righteous in God's sight, but it is those who obey the law who will be declared righteous. (Rom 2:13)

For the LORD watches over the way of the righteous, but the way of the wicked will perish. (Psa 1:6)

Then they will go away to eternal punishment, but the righteous to eternal life. (Matt 25:46)

For Christ died for sins once for all, the righteous for the unrighteous, to bring you to God. He was put to death in the body but made alive by the Spirit, (1 Peter 3:18)

What does the Scripture say? "Abraham believed God, and it was credited to him as righteousness." (Rom 4:3; Gen 15:6)

The LORD rewards every man for his righteousness and faithfulness. (1 Sam 26:23)

O LORD, God of Israel, you are righteous! (Ezra 9:15)

Therefore the wicked will not stand in the judgment, nor sinners in the assembly of the righteous. For the LORD watches over the way of the righteous, but the way of the wicked will perish. (Ps 1:5-6)

"The days are coming," declares the LORD, "when I will raise up to David a righteous Branch, a King who will reign wisely and do what is just and right in the land. In his days Judah will be saved and Israel will live in safety. This is the name by which he will be called: The LORD Our Righteousness. (Jer 23:5-6)

And you will again see the distinction between the righteous and the wicked, between those who serve God and those who do not. (Mal 3:18)

Then they [the wicked] will go away to eternal punishment, but the righteous to eternal life. (Matt 25:46)

The prayer of a righteous man is powerful and effective. (James 5:16)

We begin this section by examining the theology represented in the word, *righteous.*

However, first, we shall examine the passages at the beginning of this chapter which express truths that briefly summarize this subject.

Habakkuk 2:4 defines faith as the basis of righteousness. In addition, Habakkuk 2:4 is also the foundational passage on which Paul built his theology of the gospel in the Epistle to the Romans.

Romans 2:13 expresses the truth that obedience to God is the basis of righteousness.

Job 9:2 expresses the amazement at the holiness of God and the sinfulness of man—and wonders, in such a relationship, how can anyone be righteous before God? Although God is righteous, our righteousness will be like *filthy rags* in comparison to the righteousness of God (Isa 64:6).

Psalm 1:6 defines the relationship between God and the righteous: God watches over the way of the righteous, but the wicked will perish.

Matthew 25:46 restates the message of Daniel 12:1-4: everyone shall have eternal life: the wicked to eternal punishment and the righteous to eternal life with God.

I Peter 3:18 states that Christ, the Righteous One, died for the unrighteous to bring us to God. There is no other means of salvation, except through the Cross of Christ. *Salvation is found in no one else, for there is no other name under heaven given to men by which we must be saved. (Acts 4:12)*

Romans 4:3 expressed the relationship between believing and righteousness. Abraham is the man of faith, who believed and trusted God; therefore all who trust God and who believe in God are called righteous.

The basic conclusion is: *faith is the basis of righteousness; without faith, there is no righteousness.*

So we begin the discussion of the *message* of the gospel: *The righteous shall live by faith (Habakkuk 2:4; Romans 1:17).*

According, this chapter, and the next two, will emphasize three terms: *righteous, live,* and *faith.*

The word, *righteous,* is used 303 times in the Bible: 238 times in the Old Testament and 65 times in the New Testament. The word, *righteousness,* is used 239 times in the Bible: 159 times in the Old Testament and 80 times in the New Testament. These two words, *righteous* and *righteousness,* dominate the Old Testament in comparison to the New Testament. Therefore, *righteous* and *righteousness* are basically Old Testament doctrines, with their fullness developed and expressed in the New Testament.

Righteousness defines man's relationship with God (Psa 50:6; Jer 9:24) and with other people (Jer 22:3). In human relationships, righteous action promotes love and peace in their relationships to each other. Righteousness is holy living, according to God's standard. God's character is the definition and source of all righteousness (Gen 18:25; Deut 32:4; Rom 9:14). Therefore, man's righteousness is defined in terms of God's.

The fundamental truth is: *What does the Scripture say? "Abraham believed God, and it was credited to him as righteousness." (Rom 4:3; James 2:23)*

Belief in God is the foundation of our righteousness. The more we believe in God, the greater is our righteousness. The combination of both the Old Testament and the New Testament show man's need for righteousness. The sacrificial system in the Old Testament and the Cross of Christ in the New Testament are the keys that unlock this great mystery.

Since the original sin of man in the Garden of Eden, man is inherently wicked and evil. As the prophet Isaiah said, *All of us have become like one who is unclean, and all our righteous acts are like filthy rags; we all shrivel up like a leaf, and like the wind our sins sweep us away. (Isa 64:6)*

Our own merit is never sufficient for righteousness in the sight of God. Therefore, our righteousness depends on God's righteousness being transferred to us. That transfer occurred on the Cross of Christ, which is an eternal witness to God's love and righteousness. On the cross, God transfers the righteousness of Christ to those who trust in Him (Rom 4:3-22; Gal 3:6; Phil 3:9); in return, Christ took on our sins. We become righteous only because of our identification by faith with Jesus Christ.

Faith in Christ is the key to righteousness.

With that brief introduction, we shall examine the word, *righteous and righteousness*, on both a divine and a human level, seeking truths about God and about ourselves.

In doing so, we shall address the following questions: What is the divine nature of righteousness? What is the origin of our righteousness? Who are righteous? What is the purpose of our righteousness? What are the results of our righteousness? In like manner, what does it mean to be righteous? What is the result of our being righteous? Above all, what does being righteous have to do with our relationship with God?

These questions we now consider.

First, Righteousness on a divine level:

God is Righteous (Ezra 9:15; Psa 4:1; Isa 24:16; Isa 45:21-22); Jesus Christ honored the Father as righteous (John 17:25). God is called by the name: The Lord our Righteousness (Jer 23:6).

God is the Source of righteousness; it is apart from the law and it is received by faith in Christ Jesus (Rom 3:21-22).

The righteous God is present in the company of the righteous (Psa 14:5); God watches over the ways of the righteous (Psa 1:6). The Lord blesses and approves of the righteous (Psa 5:12). God loves the righteous (Psa 146:8); God is a shield for the righteous (Psa 5:12); God blesses the homes of the righteous (Prov 3:33). The eyes of the Lord are on the righteous, and He listens to their prayers (1 Pet 3:12). God restores the soul of the righteous, as well as guiding us into the paths of righteousness (Psa 23:3). God will make our righteousness shine like the dawn (Psa 37:6).

Because we love righteousness and hate wickedness, God has anointed the righteous with the oil of joy (Psa 45:7).

God's decrees are righteous (Rom 1:32); His judgments are righteous (Rom 2:5) God is called the righteous Judge (Psa 7:11). God comes to judge the earth in righteousness and equity (Psa 98:9); in addition, He will govern the people with justice (Psa 9:8). God is exalted by His justice and His holiness is a reflection of His righteousness (Isa 5:16). As Judge, the Lord rewards everyone for their righteousness and faithfulness (I Sam 26:23). His judgments will be based on righteousness (Psa 94:16). From the judgments of God, the nations learn righteousness (Isa 26:9-10).

The Kingdom of God is about righteousness, peace and joy in the Holy Spirit (Rom 14:17).

God is recognized as the Righteous One (Isa 24:16; Acts 3:14). In addition, God made Christ, who knew no sin, to become sin for us, so that we would become the righteousness of God (2 Cor 5:21).

Jesus Christ is equally acknowledged as the Holy and Righteous One (Acts 3:14-15; 7:52). Christ is the Righteous One who died for our sins to bring the unrighteous to God (1 Pet 3:18). If we sin, we have an Advocate with the Father, Jesus Christ, the Righteous One (1 John 2:1). The message of salvation through the Cross of Christ is that Christ's obedience is the foundation of our righteousness. If Christ is in you, you are dead to sin but alive because of righteousness (Rom 8:10). Because Christ is the end of the law, there is righteousness for all who believe (Rom 10:4).

However, concerning His Son, God said that, because you have loved righteousness and hated wickedness, God has anointed you with the oil of joy (Heb 1:8-9).

Because Christ bore our sins on the cross, we would die to sin and live for righteousness; it is by his wounds that we have been healed. (1 Peter 2:24)

We see that, through the obedience of one Man (Christ), many will be made righteous (Rom 5:18-19).

The heavens proclaim the righteousness of God and the people see His glory (Psa 97:6).

God's righteousness is eternal; His salvation is available forever (Isa 51:8).

God is eternal; always speaking in righteousness and mighty to save (Isa 63:1). God declared that, if a country sinned against God, only the truly righteous, such as Noah, Daniel, and Job, would be able to save themselves in such a time (Eze 14:12-14).

God is always prepared to rescue us from the hands of our enemies so that we can serve Him without fear in holiness and righteousness (Luke 1:74-75).

The Holy Spirit will convict everyone of sin and the need for righteousness (John 16:8-11).

Witness these truths in the following passages:

O LORD, God of Israel, you are righteous! We are left this day as a remnant. Here we are before you in our guilt, though because of it not one of us can stand in your presence. (Ezra 9:15)

Answer me when I call to you, O my righteous God. (Psa 4:1)

From the ends of the earth we hear singing: "Glory to the Righteous One." (Isa 24:16)

Was it not I, the LORD? And there is no God apart from me, a righteous God and a Savior; there is none but me. "Turn to me and be saved, all you ends of the earth; for I am God, and there is no other." (Isa 45:21-22)

Righteous Father, though the world does not know you, I [Christ] know you, and they know that you have sent me. (John 17:25)

God is a righteous judge, a God who expresses his wrath every day. (Psa 7:11)

But the LORD Almighty will be exalted by his justice, and the holy God will show himself holy by his righteousness. (Isa 5:16)

There they are, overwhelmed with dread, for God is present in the company of the righteous. (Psa 14:5)

For the LORD watches over the way of the righteous, but the way of the wicked will perish. (Psa 1:6)

For surely, O LORD, you bless the righteous; you surround them with your favor as with a shield. (Psa 5:12)

See what the Lord God does for righteous people: The eyes of the LORD are on the righteous and his ears are attentive to their cry; the face of the LORD is against those who do evil, to cut off the memory of them from the earth. The righteous cry out, and the LORD hears them; he delivers them from all their troubles. The LORD is close to the brokenhearted and saves those who are crushed in spirit. A righteous man may have many troubles, but the LORD delivers him from them all: he delivers them from all their troubles. (Psa 34:15-17)

The LORD loves the righteous. (Psa 146:8)

The Lord blesses the home of the righteous. (Prov 3:33)

For the eyes of the Lord are on the righteous and his ears are attentive to their prayer, but the face of the Lord is against those who do evil. (1 Peter 3:12)

"The days are coming," declares the LORD, *"when I will raise up to David a righteous Branch, a King who will reign wisely and do what is just and right in the land. (Jer 23:5)*

You [the Jews] disowned the Holy and Righteous One and asked that a murderer be released to you. You killed the author of life, but God raised him from the dead. (Acts 3:14-15)

Although they know God's righteous decree (Rom 1:32)...when his righteous judgment will be revealed. God will give to each person according to what he has done." (Rom 2:5-6)

But if Christ is in you, your body is dead because of sin, yet your spirit is alive because of righteousness. (Rom 8:10)

For Christ died for sins once for all, the righteous [Christ] for the unrighteous, to bring you to God. (1 Peter 3:18)

But if anybody does sin, we have one who speaks to the Father in our defense — Jesus Christ, the Righteous One. (1 John 2:1)

He who is coming [Jesus Christ] will come and will not delay. But my righteous one will live by faith. (Heb 10:37-38)

Hallelujah! For our Lord God Almighty reigns. Let us rejoice and be glad and give him glory! For the wedding of the Lamb has come, and his bride has made herself ready. Fine linen, bright and clean, was given her to wear. (Fine linen stands for the <u>righteous acts of the saints</u>.) (Rev 19:6-8)

The heavens proclaim his righteousness, and all the peoples see his glory. (Psa 97:6)

For he [God] comes to judge the earth. He will judge the world in righteousness and the peoples with equity. (Psa 98:9)

This is the name by which he [God] will be called: The LORD Our Righteousness. (Jer 23:6)

The LORD rewards every man for his righteousness and faithfulness. (1 Sam 26:23)

He [God] will judge the world in righteousness; he will govern the peoples with justice. (Psa 9:8)

He [God] restores my soul. He guides me in paths of righteousness for his name's sake. (Psa 23:3)

He will make your righteousness shine like the dawn, the justice of your cause like the noonday sun. (Psa 37:6)

You love righteousness and hate wickedness; therefore God, your God, has set you above your companions by anointing you with the oil of joy. (Psa 45:7)

Judgment will again be founded on righteousness, and all the upright in heart will follow it. (Psa 94:15)

When your [God's] judgments come upon the earth, the people of the world learn righteousness. Though grace is shown to the wicked, they do not learn righteousness; (Isa 26:9-10)

Who is this coming from Edom, from Bozrah, with his garments stained crimson? Who is this, robed in splendor, striding forward in the greatness of his strength? "It is I [God], speaking in righteousness, mighty to save." (Isa 63:1)

The word of the LORD came to me: "Son of man, if a country sins against me by being unfaithful and I stretch out my hand against it to cut off its food supply and send famine upon it and kill its men and their animals, even if these three men — Noah, Daniel and Job — were in it, they could save only themselves by their righteousness, declares the Sovereign LORD. (Ezek 14:12-14)

To rescue us from the hand of our enemies, and to enable us to serve him without fear in holiness and righteousness before him all our days. (Luke 1:74-75)

When he [the Holy Spirit] comes, he will convict the world of guilt in regard to sin and righteousness and judgment: in regard to sin, because men do not believe in me; in regard to righteousness, because I am going to the Father, where you can see me no longer; and in regard to judgment, because the prince of this world now stands condemned. (John 16:8-11)

But now a righteousness from God, apart from law, has been made known, to which the Law and the Prophets testify. This righteousness from God comes through faith in Jesus Christ to all who believe. (Rom 3:21-22)

Consequently, just as the result of one trespass was condemnation for all men, so also the result of one act of righteousness was justification that brings life for all men. For just as through the disobedience of the one man the many were made sinners, so also through the obedience of the one man the many will be made righteous. (Rom 5:18-19)

Christ is the end of the law so that there may be righteousness for everyone who believes. (Rom 10:4)

For the kingdom of God is not a matter of eating and drinking, but of righteousness, peace and joy in the Holy Spirit, because anyone who serves Christ in this way is pleasing to God and approved by men. (Rom 14:17-18)

God made him [Christ] who had no sin to be sin for us, so that in him we might become the righteousness of God. (2 Cor 5:21)

But about the Son he [God] says, "Your throne, O God, will last forever and ever, and righteousness will be the scepter of your kingdom. You have loved righteousness and hated wickedness; therefore God, your God, has set you above your companions by anointing you with the oil of joy." (Heb 1:8-9)

He himself bore our sins in his body on the tree, so that we might die to sins and live for righteousness; by his wounds you have been healed. (1 Peter 2:24)

Now, consider righteousness from a human perspective.

Second, Righteousness on a human level

We are to recognize that righteousness comes from God; righteousness is not by the law, but by faith in Christ Jesus (Rom 3:21-22).

Now, we address the characteristics of a righteous person which are based on belief/faith in God (Gen 15:6). We continue to see the righteousness that comes from faith (Rom 4:13).

The first righteous person identified in Scripture was Noah whose righteousness was evident because he *walked* with God (Gen 6:9). Noah went where God went; he did what God did; he obeyed God. That is the evidence of his righteousness, and it is the evidence that the righteous live by faith (Heb 10:37). Noah became the heir of righteousness that comes by faith (Heb 11:7). As with Noah, Abraham's faith was credited to him as righteousness (Rom 4:9).

Consider other evidence of a righteous person. He speaks the truth; he does not commit slander; he honors those who reverence God (Psa 15:2-4). He serves and obeys God (Mal 3:18); he speaks with justice. He has the laws of God in his heart, and he obeys the commandments of God (Rom 2:13-14). The righteous speak wisdom from God (Psa 37:30-31). Therefore, God approved and blesses those who hunger and thirst after righteousness (Matt 5:6); God also blesses those who are persecuted for righteousness' sake (Matt 5:10). In addition, we are encouraged to seek first His kingdom and His righteousness (Matt 6:33).

The righteous will receive a crown of beauty; they will be called oaks of righteousness, a planting of the Lord to display His splendor (Isa 61:3). As a result of their actions, the righteous will be listed in the Book of Life (Psa 69:26).

The result of a righteous life is that they will shine like the sun in God's kingdom (Matt 13:43). In addition, they will receive the crown of righteousness (2 Tim 4:8). The prayers of the righteous man are powerful and effective (James 5:16). In life (salvation), there is immortality for the righteous man (Prov 12:28). The rewards of following righteousness are life (salvation), prosperity, and honor (Prov 21:21). The fruit of righteousness is peace, quietness, and confidence forever (Isa 32:17).

We look forward to a new heaven, a new earth, and a new Jerusalem, the City of God, which will be called the City of Righteousness, when it honors and worships God (Isa 1:2; 2 Pet 3:13).

By the grace of God, we know that righteousness came, not through the law, but through faith (Gal 2:21). It is through the Spirit that we await the righteousness for which we hope (Gal 5:5). We are to put on the new self, created to be like God in true righteousness and holiness (Eph 4:22-23). We are not to seek a righteousness that comes through the law, but a true righteousness that comes from God and is by faith (Phil 3:8-9).

Further, we know that the Scriptures are God-breathed and that they are invaluable for training in righteousness (2 Tim 3:16-17).

Witness these truths in the following passages.

Abram believed the LORD, and he credited it to him as righteousness. (Gen 15:6)

Noah was a righteous man, blameless among the people of his time, and he walked with God. (Gen 6:9)

He whose walk is blameless and who does what is righteous, who speaks the truth from his heart and has no slander on his tongue, who does his neighbor no wrong and casts no slur on his fellowman, who despises a vile man but honors those who fear the LORD, who keeps his oath even when it hurts, (Psa 15:2-4)

Nevertheless, the righteous will hold to their ways, and those with clean hands will grow stronger. (Job 17:9)

The mouth of the righteous man utters wisdom, and his tongue speaks what is just. The law of his God is in his heart; his feet do not slip. (Psa 37:30-31)

May they [the wicked] be blotted out of the book of life and not be listed with the righteous. (Psa 69:28)

And you will again see the distinction between the righteous and the wicked, between those who serve God and those who do not. (Mal 3:18)

Then the righteous will shine like the sun in the kingdom of their Father. He who has ears, let him hear. (Matt 13:43)

For it is not those who hear the law who are righteous in God's sight, but it is those who obey the law who will be declared righteous. (Rom 2:13-14)

Now there is in store for me the crown of righteousness, which the Lord, the righteous Judge, will award to me on that day — and not only to me, but also to all who have longed for his appearing. (2 Tim 4:8)

The prayer of a righteous man is powerful and effective. (James 5:16)

In the way of righteousness there is life; along that path is immortality. (Prov 12:28)

The LORD detests the way of the wicked but he loves those who pursue righteousness. (Prov 15:9)

He who pursues righteousness and love finds life, prosperity and honor. (Prov 21:21)

Afterward you [Jerusalem] will be called the City of Righteousness, the Faithful City. (Isa 1:2)

The fruit of righteousness will be peace; the effect of righteousness will be quietness and confidence forever. (Isa 32:17)

But my [God's] righteousness will last forever, my salvation through all generations. (Isa 51:8)

He put on righteousness as his breastplate, and the helmet of salvation on his head; he put on the garments of vengeance and wrapped himself in zeal as in a cloak. (Isa 59:17)

To bestow on them a crown of beauty instead of ashes, the oil of gladness instead of mourning, and a garment of praise instead of a spirit of despair. They will be called oaks of righteousness, a planting of the LORD for the display of his splendor. (Isa 61:3)

But in keeping with his promise we are looking forward to a new heaven and a new earth, the home of righteousness [the New Jerusalem]. (2 Peter 3:13)

Blessed are those who hunger and thirst for righteousness, for they shall be filled. (Matt 5:6)

Blessed are those who are persecuted because of righteousness, for theirs is the kingdom of heaven. (Matt 5:10)

But seek first his kingdom and his righteousness, and all these things will be given to you as well. (Matt 6:33)

But now a righteousness from God, apart from law, has been made known, to which the Law and the Prophets testify. This righteousness from God comes through faith in Jesus Christ to all who believe. (Rom 3:21-22)

However, to the man who does not work but trusts God who justifies the wicked, his faith is credited as righteousness. David says the same thing when he speaks of the blessedness of the man to whom God credits righteousness apart from works: "Blessed are they whose transgressions are forgiven, whose sins are covered. Blessed is the man whose sin the Lord will never count against him." (Rom 4:5-8)

We have been saying that Abraham's faith was credited to him as righteousness (Rom 4:9)

through the righteousness that comes by faith. (Rom 4:13)

Moses describes in this way the righteousness that is by the law: "The man who does these things will live by them." But the righteousness that is by faith says: "Do not say in your heart, 'Who will ascend into heaven?'" (that is, to bring Christ down) "or 'Who will descend into the deep?'" (that is, to bring Christ up from the dead). But what does it say? "The word is near you; it is in your mouth and in your heart," that is, the word of faith we are proclaiming: That if you confess with your mouth, "Jesus is Lord," and believe in your heart that God raised him from the dead, you will be saved. For it is with your heart that you believe and are justified, and it is with your mouth that you confess and are saved. (Rom 10:5-10)

It is because of him that you are in Christ Jesus, who has become for us wisdom from God — that is, our righteousness, holiness and redemption. (1 Cor 1:30)

I [Paul] do not set aside the grace of God, for if righteousness could be gained through the law, Christ died for nothing! (Gal 2:21)

But by faith we eagerly await through the Spirit the righteousness for which we hope. (Gal 5:5-6)

You were taught, with regard to your former way of life, to put off your old self, which is being corrupted by its deceitful desires; to be made new in the attitude of your minds; and to put on the new self, created to be like God in true righteousness and holiness. (Eph 4:22-24)

I [Paul] consider them rubbish, that I may gain Christ and be found in him, not having a righteousness of my own that comes from the law, but that which is through faith in Christ — the righteousness that comes from God and is by faith. (Phil 3:8-9)

All Scripture is God-breathed and is useful for teaching, rebuking, correcting and training in righteousness, so that the man of God may be thoroughly equipped for every good work. (2 Tim 3:16-17)

I have fought the good fight, I have finished the race, I have kept the faith. Now there is in store for me the crown of righteousness, which the Lord, the righteous Judge, will award to me on that day — and not only to me, but also to all who have longed for his appearing. (2 Tim 4:7-8)

By faith Noah, when warned about things not yet seen, in holy fear built an ark to save his family. By his faith he condemned the world and became heir of the righteousness that comes by faith. (Heb 11:7)

But in keeping with his promise we are looking forward to a new heaven and a new earth, the home of righteousness. (2 Peter 3:13)

Before concluding, it is necessary to consider one question: do the righteous ever falter and fail to be righteous? The answer is yes. Consider Abraham, Moses, David, and the apostle Peter. These certainly were righteous men. Yet consider certain events in their lives.

First, consider *Abraham*. There are at least two events which show the unrighteousness and unfaithfulness of Abraham. The first was the deceit involved in claiming Sarah, his wife, as his sister (Gen 12:12-16).

When the Egyptians see you [Sarah], they will say, 'This is his wife.' Then they will kill me [Abraham] but will let you live. Say you are my sister, so that I will be treated well for your sake and my life will be spared because of you." When Abram came to Egypt, the Egyptians saw that she was a very beautiful woman. And when Pharaoh's officials saw her, they praised her to Pharaoh, and she was taken into his palace. He treated Abram well for her sake, and Abram acquired sheep and cattle, male and female donkeys, menservants and maidservants, and camels. (Gen 12:12-16)

The second incident involved Abraham's and Sarah's impatience with the promise of God, that all the nations of the earth would be blessed through his offspring (Gen 22:18). After waiting ten years for God to fulfill his promise to give them a son, Abraham and Sarah decided to have Hagar, the Egyptian bondwoman of Sarah, conceive a son, Ishmael, to Abraham (Gen 16). As a result, they produced an offspring, which was not according to the will of God. This act demonstrated disobedience on Abraham's part as well as a lack of faith in God. God's will was for a supernatural offspring, because God had planned that Abraham and Sarah would be well past the age when human conception could occur. The offspring was to represent a divine act, not a human one.

Moses: During the Exodus, Moses' patience was continually tested by the murmurings, grumblings, and complaints of the people. At one point, Moses' lost all patience, and he sinned against the Lord. When the people grumbled against Moses, saying they had no water, God told Moses to *speak* to the rock and water would flow forth. Instead of obeying God, Moses lifted his hand and struck the rock twice with his rod and water came forth. Because of his disobedience, Moses was not permitted to enter the Promised Land (Num 20:1-13). That privilege would belong to his successor, Joshua.

David: David was a righteous king; but he was open to temptation. Once when his army went to battle, David remained in Jerusalem. David observed Bathsheba bathing, and he was struck by her beauty. As a result, David committed adultery with Bathsheba. When David discovered that Bathsheba was pregnant, David had Uriah, the Hittite, Bathsheba's husband, returned from the battle lines so that he could sleep with his wife and the child could be declared the child of Uriah. However, Uriah refused to do so, and David was faced with a further dilemma. Therefore, in an effort to cover this sin of adultery, David commanded that Uriah be placed in the front line during the battle, so it would be certain that he would be killed. David added the sin of murder to the sin of adultery. Later David was confronted by the prophet Nathan, regarding his double sins. As a result, David repented and sought God's forgiveness (Psalm 51).

Consider the apostle *Peter:* Peter continually expressed his love and faithfulness to Jesus Christ, in spite of the dangers and difficulties that might arise. However, Jesus understood the frail nature of the human spirit. *"I tell you the truth,"* *Jesus answered, "this very night, before the rooster crows, you will disown me three times."* But Peter declared, *"Even if I have to die with you, I will never disown you."* And all the other disciples said the same. *(Matt 26:34-35)*

Jesus is arrested and taken before the High Priest, Caiaphas, then before Herod and the Roman authorities. Crowds were waiting to hear the judgment. In the midst of the crowds was Peter, who was challenged by those in the crowd.

After a little while, those standing there went up to Peter and said, "Surely you are one of them, for your accent gives you away." Then he began to call down curses on himself and he swore to them, "I don't know the man!" Immediately a rooster crowed. Then Peter remembered the word Jesus had spoken: "Before the rooster crows, you will disown me three times." And he went outside and wept bitterly. (Matt 26:73-75)

Peter tried to hide in the crowd; but, when challenged, Peter said: *I don't know the man!*

What a denial!

I bring these examples up, because no one is perfect and no one can faithfully sustain a life of pure and continuous righteousness. When they stumbled, God picked them up. When we stumble, God will pick us up.

We conclude.

The righteous are those who believe and trust in God.

In addition, the righteous are those who love God, who love their neighbors, who acknowledge God as God, who seek to know the will and the purposes of God, who seek to do the will of God, who are faithful in all respects, and who seek to glorify God by all that they do and by all that they say. The righteous are Christ-centered, Spirit-filled, Bible-believing, people of prayer, the salt of the earth and the light of the world.

God's character and actions are the definition of righteousness (Gen 18:25; Deut 32:4; Rom 9:14). As a result, man's righteousness is defined in terms of God's.

When man does that which is consistent with the character of God, then man takes on the very nature of the righteousness of God.

Chapter 12

*The righteous shall **live** by faith (Rom 1:17)*

Multitudes who sleep in the dust of the earth will awake: some to everlasting life, others to shame and everlasting contempt. (Dan 12:2-3)

Then they will go away to eternal punishment, but the righteous to eternal life. (Matt 25:46)

Whoever believes in the Son has eternal life, but whoever rejects the Son will not see life, for God's wrath remains on him. (John 3:36)

No one has seen the Father except the one who is from God; only he has seen the Father. I [Christ] tell you the truth, he who believes has everlasting life. (John 6:46-47)

Jesus said, "For judgment I have come into this world, so that the blind will see and those who see will become blind." (John 9:39)

I [Jesus Christ] have come that they may have life, and have it to the full. (John 10:10)

I [Jesus Christ] have come into the world as a light, so that no one who believes in me should stay in darkness. (John 12:46)

We now address the understanding that *to live* is to be considered as to *be saved*.

Therefore the passage, Romans 1:17, can also be translated: *the righteous will be saved by faith.*

In Scripture, *life* is *salvation*. Jesus said: I have come to give you life: I have come to save you.

However, the life that Christ is referring to is not this physical life with all of its human dimensions and limitations.

No, Christ has come so that we would experience the spiritual life that the Father enjoys and that the Son enjoys. *God is spirit, and his worshipers must worship in spirit and in truth. (John 4:24)*

As God is Spirit, so does He call us to be spiritual. He calls us to be born spiritually; He calls us to live spiritually; He calls us to seek the things that are above; He calls us to live by the Spirit and to walk by the Spirit and to be led into all truth by the Spirit; He calls us to grow in the Spirit so that we can grow into the image of God, for which we were created.

We are spiritual people in a physical body.

The spiritual life is the resurrected life.

The spiritual life is eternal life.

That is the life that Jesus Christ came to give us.

He came to give us this spiritual life so that we would seek the things that are above, in the heavenly realm.

He has come to give us this spiritual life so that we would be born again, know God as our Heavenly Father, and be His children.

Let us begin by examining the passages at the beginning of this chapter because they shed light on our subject.

The first passage (Dan 12:2-3) is the first biblical evidence that everyone will have eternal life. However, the questions are: where will it be spent? Will it be the eternal life with God? Or will it be eternal life filled with shame and everlasting contempt?

The second passage (Matt 25:46) presents the New Testament truth expressed by Jesus Christ that there will be separation with the righteous having eternal life, but the wicked facing eternal punishment.

The third passage (John 3:36) contains the truth that the acceptance/rejection of Jesus Christ determines whether a person will share eternal life with God. The acceptance/rejection of Jesus Christ also determines whether a person will receive the love or wrath of God.

The fourth passage (John 6:46-47) states that faith in God is the basis for everlasting life.

The fifth passage (John 9:39) states one of the reasons that Christ came into the world: that judgment will come to all people and that the spiritually blind will become physically blind.

The sixth passage (John 10:10) states another of the reasons that Christ came into the world which was to bring salvation to all those who would believe in the Son.

The seventh passage (John 12:46) states a further reason that Christ came into the world, which was to bring light to a world in darkness and to rescue us from this present evil age (Gal. 1:1-3). To be in the light is to be saved; to be in the darkness is to experience eternal condemnation.

So what does it mean to *live* and what does it mean to have eternal life or everlasting life?

Eternal life refers to our redeemed existence in Jesus Christ which is granted by God as a gift to all believers. The phrase, everlasting life, is found in the Old Testament only once (Dan 12:2). But the idea of eternal life is implied by the prophets in their pictures of the glorious future promised to God's people. The majority of references to eternal life in the New Testament are oriented towards the future. The emphasis, however, is upon the glorious character of the life that will be enjoyed endlessly in the future. Jesus emphasized that eternal life comes only to those who make a total commitment to Him (Matt 19:16-21; Luke 18:18-22).

Now a man came up to Jesus and asked, "Teacher, what good thing must I do to get eternal life?" "Why do you ask me about what is *good?" Jesus replied. "There is only One who is good. If you want to enter life, obey the commandments." "Which ones?" the man inquired. Jesus replied, "'Do not murder, do not commit adultery, do not steal, do not give false testimony, honor your father and mother,' and 'love your neighbor as yourself.'" "All these I have kept," the young man said. "What do I still lack?" Jesus answered, "If you want to be perfect, go, sell your possessions and give to the poor, and you will have treasure in heaven. <u>Then come, follow me</u>." When the young man heard this, he went away sad, because he had great wealth. (Matt 19:16-22)*

This passage warrants further examination.

The young man probably was earnestly seeking eternal life. At least, he asked the question; at least, he showed a certain degree of interest. Many people don't even ask the question. In response to Jesus' response and question, he believed that he had been faithful in keeping the commandments, but now Jesus went beyond the commandments and the law. Jesus said that eternal life is based on having a personal relationship with Christ. If anyone wants to have eternal life, then they must follow Jesus. Jesus invited the young man to trade his earthly and physical wealth for the spiritual treasures in heaven. To do so required that the young man sell his earthly wealth and follow Jesus Christ. Spiritual treasures are found only in a relationship with Christ. The young man was sad because the wealth of this world was more important to him than the wealth and treasures in heaven. The key to eternal life is following Jesus Christ. But what does that mean and what does it entail? Well, it means to follow Christ's example, to follow His lifestyle, to follow His example of the relationship with God the Father, to have the character of Christ, to have the mind of Christ, to have the vision of Christ, to seek the treasures of Christ, to love the Father as Christ loves the Father, to love our neighbor as Christ loved His neighbor. Above all else, it means to seek the things that are above, not the things of this earth. Our vision is to be heaven-directed; our life is to seek the spiritual rather than the physical. It means to love as Christ loved; it means to be willing to die physically so that we can live spiritually. It means to be *crucified with Christ*. That is the vision that Paul had for his life.

I have been crucified with Christ and I no longer live, but Christ lives in me. The life I live in the body, I live by faith in the Son of God, who loved me and gave himself for me. (Gal 2:20)

When we can do that, then Jesus said: we will *inherit* eternal life.

Let us now examine three passages from the epistles of Paul regarding the doctrine of eternal life: Romans 5:20-22, 6:22-23, and Galatians 6:8.

The law was added so that the trespass might increase. But where sin increased, grace increased all the more, so that, just as sin reigned in death, so also grace might reign through righteousness to bring eternal life through Jesus Christ our Lord. (Rom 5:20-22).

This passage has three important truths. The *first truth* is that the law was given to define sin. In fact, the Scriptures say that *sin is lawlessness* (I John 3:4). But then we have this great truth in John 1:17: *For the law was given through Moses; grace and truth came through Jesus Christ.* The *second truth* is that sin leads to spiritual death which is spiritual separation from God. Sin is the measure of our disobedience to God; death is not physical death but spiritual death. The *third truth* is that grace is God's love for the sinners and God's grace leads to our righteousness (which is faith in God) and that faith in God leads to eternal life through the Cross of Jesus Christ.

Consider the second passage from the Apostle Paul. Here Paul repeated some of the truths which he stated in the previous passage.

But now that you have been set free from sin and have become slaves to God, the benefit you reap leads to holiness, and the result is eternal life. For the wages of sin is death, but the gift of God is eternal life in Christ Jesus our Lord. (Rom 6:22-23)

This passage is similar to what Paul had written 7 years earlier in the Epistle to the Galatians in which Paul stressed the truth that; *It is for freedom that Christ has set us free. Stand firm, then, and do not let yourselves be burdened again by a yoke of slavery. (Gal 5:1).* In the Roman passage, Paul reiterated that Christians are set free from sin and have become slaves to God. The benefit of that exchange is holiness: the result is eternal life. If we are a slave to sin, the result is spiritual death which is eternal separation from God. If we are a slave to God, the result is eternal life with God. The alternatives are clear. Sin leads to separation; holiness leads to union with God.

The third passage from Paul is equally instructive in stating the alternatives in life and the conditions that lead to eternal life.

The one who sows to please his sinful nature, from that nature will reap destruction; the one who sows to please the Spirit, from the Spirit will reap eternal life. (Gal 6:8)

In this passage, Paul outlines the truth that what we sow is what we will reap. If a person sows to his sinful nature, he will reap destruction. However, if a person sows to please the Spirit of God, that person will reap eternal life.

The phrase, eternal life, does not appear in the Old Testament and appears 42 times in the New Testament, most often in the Gospel of John (16 times) and the Epistle of 1 John (6 times). Because of the preponderance of attention to eternal life in these two documents, I will focus primarily on them in this discussion of eternal life. We begin with the recognition that John emphasized eternal life as the present reality and the present possession of the Christian. John declared that the Christian believer has already begun to experience the blessings of the future now, even before their fullest expression will occur in the Age to come.

Just as Moses lifted up the snake in the desert, so the Son of Man must be lifted up, that everyone who believes in him may have eternal life. (John 3:14-15)

This event is foreshadowed during the Exodus (*Num 21:4-9*), at which time the Israelites grumbled against God and against Moses. So the LORD sent venomous snakes among them, and many Israelites died. The people acknowledged their sin, and they asked Moses to pray that the LORD will take the snakes away from them. So, as a result of Moses' prayer, the LORD told Moses, *Make a snake and put it up on a pole; anyone who is bitten can look at it and live. So Moses made a bronze snake and put it up on a pole. Then when anyone was bitten by a snake and looked at the bronze snake, he lived.*

It is this episode which the Apostle John had in mind when he recorded the words of Jesus: *Just as Moses lifted up the snake in the desert, so the Son of Man must be lifted up, that everyone who believes in him may have eternal life.* Here again we have the foundation for eternal life: it is to *believe* in Jesus Christ. It is to have faith in what He has done to secure our redemption and reconciliation with God.

Whoever believes in the Son has eternal life, but whoever rejects the Son will not see life, for God's wrath remains on him. (John 3:36)

Again this passage stressed the necessity of *faith (belief)* in Christ as the basis of eternal life. If we believe now, we have eternal life now. However, this passage also stated that rejection of the Son of God will mean two things: first, that person will not have eternal life; second, God's wrath remains on him.

I tell you the truth, whoever hears my word and believes him who sent me has eternal life and will not be condemned; he has crossed over from death to life. (John 5:24)

Again, we have the words of Jesus Christ in which He now stressed the necessity to *hear* His words, which means to *obey* what He has commanded. Obedience is the evidence of hearing. So here we have the dual requirements to be *obedient* and *believe in God* as two conditions for having eternal life. Eternal life produces the following result: a person has crossed over from *death*, separation from God, to *life*, reconciliation with God.

Now this is eternal life: that they may know you, the only true God, and Jesus Christ, whom you have sent. (John 17:3)

In this passage, Christ stated the present reality of eternal life which is *knowledge of God* and *union with God*. But there is an important coupling here and that is between God *and* Jesus Christ. Christ said: it is equally important to know and be in union with Jesus Christ as the One sent from God and who is the revelation of God.

I [John] write these things to you who believe in the name of the Son of God so that you may know that you have eternal life. (1 John 5:13)

The Apostle John now identifies to *believe in the name of the Son of God* as the foundational condition for having eternal life. So what does it mean to *believe in the name* of Jesus Christ?

We must understand what the name of God truly means. The name of the Lord is synonymous with His presence: *For your wondrous works declare that your name is near (Ps 75:1)*. To know the name of God is to know God Himself (Ps 91:14). For this reason, to *take the name of the Lord your God in vain (Exo 20:7)* is to act in any way that is inconsistent with the profession of faith that He is the Lord God.

This theme is further revealed in Acts 4:7-12, when John and Peter are brought before the Sanhedrin. Recall that Peter and John had just healed a lame man, crippled from birth. A crowd came running to witness this miraculous healing. Peter explained to the crowd: *It is Jesus' name and the faith that comes through him that has given this complete healing to him, as you can all see. (Acts 3:16)*

Then both men began to teach of the resurrection of Jesus, which greatly aroused the suspicion and concern of the Sanhedrin. *They [the Sanhedrin] were greatly disturbed because the apostles were teaching the people and proclaiming in Jesus the resurrection of the dead. (Acts 4:2)*

Consider the dialogue. *They [the Sanhedrin] had Peter and John brought before them and began to question them: "By what power or what name did you do this?" Then Peter, filled with the Holy Spirit, said to them: "Rulers and elders of the people! If we are being called to account today for an act of kindness shown to a cripple and are asked how he was healed, then know this, you and all the people of Israel: It is by the name of Jesus Christ of Nazareth, whom you crucified but whom God raised from the dead, that this man stands before you healed....Salvation is found in no one else, for there is no other name under heaven given to men by which we must be saved."*

Paul captured the sense of the power in the name of Jesus in Philippians 2:9-11. *Therefore God exalted him to the highest place and gave him the name that is above every name, that at the name of Jesus every knee should bow, in heaven and on earth and under the earth, and every tongue confess that Jesus Christ is Lord, to the glory of God the Father. (Phil 2:9-11)*

When we believe in *His name*, we believe in *His Presence*. His Presence is the basis of believing in His omnipotence, omnipresence, and omniscience. The Son of God is truly God the Son.

And so, we have an understanding of what it means to *live*. To *live* means to be *saved*; to *live* means to have *eternal life*.

We now address the final truth in the gospel message: *the righteous shall live by faith.*

Chapter 13

The righteous shall live by *faith* (Rom 1:17)

Now faith is the assurance of things hoped for, the conviction of things not seen (Heb 11:1 RSV)

This righteousness from God comes through faith in Jesus Christ to all who believe. There is no difference, for all have sinned and fall short of the glory of God, and are justified freely by his grace through the redemption that came by Christ Jesus. (Rom 3:22-25)

For it is by grace you have been saved, through faith — and this not from yourselves, it is the gift of God— not by works, so that no one can boast. For we are God's workmanship, created in Christ Jesus to do good works, which God prepared in advance for us to do. (Eph 2:8-10)

Consider it pure joy, my brothers, whenever you face trials of many kinds, because you know that the testing of your faith develops perseverance. Perseverance must finish its work so that you may be mature and complete, not lacking anything. (James 1:2-4)

We begin by examining the passages at the beginning of this chapter. The first passage (Heb 11:1) defines faith as *assurance* and *conviction*.

The second passage (Rom 3:22-25) contains three important truths: the first is that we receive righteousness from God through faith in Christ Jesus. The second truth is that all have sinned and fall short of the glory of God; the third truth is that we are declared innocent (justified) by God's grace that came through the redemption of sinners by the death of Jesus Christ on the Cross.

The third passage (Eph 2:8-10) contains the three doctrines of salvation: *grace, faith,* and *saved.* It is by God's grace and our response in faith that we are saved. His grace is a free gift. Further, we are God's workmanship, created in Christ to do good works, which God has prepared in advance for us to do. This is the statement that our tomorrows are already planned by God; all we have to do is show up for His work to be done through us and to bring Him glory.

The fourth passage (James 1:2-4) encourages us to count it pure joy when we face any trials, because such trials test our faith and develop perseverance for the life that lies ahead. James tells us that faith untested may be no faith at all. Trials are to teach and to test.

So what is this faith that comes from Christ, that is essential for salvation, that we are to count as pure joy when our faith is tested, and which must be accompanied by godly deeds in order for our faith to be counted as genuine?

Faith is the belief that is placed in a person or thing, the assurance of the truth, the conviction that we express in the way we live and the way that we witness to our Savior and Lord. Faith means to trust, to rely upon a person or idea, to participate in a self-surrendering fellowship with God and with each other. Faith is to have an assured and unwavering confidence in God. It is to state as Job did: *I know that you can do all things; no plan of yours can be thwarted. (Job 42:2)*

Faith also expresses love and loyalty to the one in whom we believe; it also involves being obedient and faithful to the person. It is a measure of our confidence and trust in God.

However, there are at least four types of faith: e.g. *saving faith, sanctifying faith, obedient faith, and serving faith* as essential for the Christian life.

Saving faith is the total confidence in God's promises and provisions in Christ for the salvation of sinners. It leads us to trust solely in the Person and work of Jesus Christ (Ephesians 2:8–10). Such faith gives the believer an unchangeable and eternal position described as being *in Christ* (Romans 8:1, Ephesians 1:3). To be *in Christ* is to be as a branch attached to Christ, the True Vine (John 15:5-8). Because of faith, believers are the *saints of God* because God has redeemed them out of darkness and brought them into His marvelous light. *Saving faith* is the confidence that we have been justified by the cross, that our sins are forgiven, that we have received the righteousness of Christ, that we receive the gift of the Spirit, and that we have become a child of God. Saving faith expresses a confidence and assurance in a personal relationship with God.

Sanctifying faith ensures growth in holiness and righteousness; it prepares us to be *set apart* for the work of God. It is the evidence of our trust in our position as being *in Christ* (Romans 6:1-10). Sanctifying faith appropriates the power of God to do what is pleasing in the sight of God. All believers are called to be sanctified (1 Corinthians 1:2), and by faith are to demonstrate their sanctification by living a godly and righteous life (Ephesians 4:1, Colossians 3:1-4).

Obedient faith is that in which work is the evidence of faith; it is to be done joyfully, generously, and willingly. It is obedience to God, living according to His commandments and living by the power of the Spirit to receive the abundant life that God alone can give His children.

Job is the obedient witness to the presence and power of God in our lives. Consider the four actions that Job has treasured; here is a witness and an example for us. *My feet have closely followed his steps; I have kept to his way without turning aside. I have not departed from the commands of his lips; I have treasured the words of his mouth more than my daily bread. (Job 23:11-12)*

Serving faith acts on the truth of both divinely bestowed spiritual gifts (I Corinthians 12:1-14:12) and fruit (Galatians 5:22) and maintains confidence in God's divine appointment for service. Here we witness to the fact that God will both convert and commission His people. He will not convert without commissioning. *For we are God's workmanship, created in Christ Jesus to do good works, which God prepared in advance for us to do. (Eph 2:10).* Here again we see the connection of being *created in Christ* to do the good works which God has prepared in advance for us to do.

This faith is fulfilled in good works. James reminds us that faith without works is dead. The essential faith/belief is that Jesus is the Christ, the Son of the Living God.

However, in a scriptural sense, faith in its larger context represents four principal ideas. The first is personal confidence in God; second, it believes in the essential body of revealed truth (Luke 18:8); third, faithfulness is evidence of the believer's trust in God; fourth, Christ is the object of faith (Galatians 3:23–25). Therefore, faith reveals trust in God, His revealed truths, the confidence we have in His promises, and Christ as the object of our faith and acknowledging fully that Jesus Christ is God Incarnate.

Again, faith is expressed by our actions/thoughts that occur *in his name, into his name, bearing his name, and through his name.* There is a uniqueness here that is important to understand. Here we focus on two words, *in* and *into,* because they have a distinctive meaning in regard to our relationship with Jesus Christ. The primary meaning of *in* is that of rest in a place or a thing. It can imply cooperation with; it can also mean on behalf of; it implies certain eagerness. Therefore, *in the name of Christ* means in union with, in cooperation with, and on behalf of Christ. On the other hand, *into* implies direction under, proceeding from, along with, beneath, but not separated from. Here the sense is that we are moving towards Christ at all times, that we are never separated from Him, and we acknowledge and are obedient to all that He commands. *In His name* is distinct from *into His name.* When baptized, we are baptized *in His name (Matthew 28:19)* which means that the sacrament is according to His power and authority. He is the Baptizer. When we are baptized, we acknowledge Christ as Savior and Lord. We accept the authority of Jesus, not just as Savior, but now as Lord of our lives.

The name of God is indicative of His character which has both transferable and non-transferable attributes. His non-transferable character is His omnipotence, omniscience, and omnipresence; these are reserved for God alone. His transferable attributes are those reflected in the Fruit of the Spirit (Gal 5:22).

The name of God also reflects His sovereignty, His authority, His majesty, His glory, His will, His purpose, and His activities. Therefore, several important names of God identify Him as the *Branch of Righteousness (Jeremiah 23:5–6); as King (Matthew 5:35); as Shepherd (Ezekiel 34:11–16); as Glory (Shekinah)*. The name of God is that represented by salvation, holiness, hope, love, baptism, forgiveness of sins, and protection by the power of His name. There are 16 names of God reflected in the Scriptures, including *El, Elohim, Yahweh,* and *Jehovah*.

There is no greater statement on faith than that contained in the 11th chapter of the Epistle to the Hebrews. This passage is of unmatched brilliance.

Now faith is being sure of what we hope for and certain of what we do not see. This is what the ancients were commended for. By faith we understand that the universe was formed at God's command, so that what is seen was not made out of what was visible. By faith Abel offered God a better sacrifice than Cain did. By faith he was commended as a righteous man, when God spoke well of his offerings. And by faith he still speaks, even though he is dead. By faith Enoch was taken from this life, so that he did not experience death; he could not be found, because God had taken him away. For before he was taken, he was commended as one who pleased God.

And without faith it is impossible to please God, because anyone who comes to him must believe that he exists and that he rewards those who earnestly seek him.

By faith Noah, when warned about things not yet seen, in holy fear built an ark to save his family. By his faith he condemned the world and became heir of the righteousness that comes by faith. By faith Abraham, when called to go to a place he would later receive as his inheritance, obeyed and went, even though he did not know where he was going. By faith he made his home in the promised land like a stranger in a foreign country; he lived in tents, as did Isaac and Jacob, who were heirs with him of the same promise. For he was looking forward to the city with foundations, whose architect and builder is God.

By faith Abraham, even though he was past age — and Sarah herself was barren — was enabled to become a father because he considered him faithful who had made the promise. And so from this one man, and he as good as dead, came descendants as numerous as the stars in the sky and as countless as the sand on the seashore.

All these people were still living by faith when they died. They did not receive the things promised; they only saw them and welcomed them from a distance. And they admitted that they were aliens and strangers on earth. People who say such things show that they are looking for a country of their own. If they had been thinking of the country they had left, they would have had opportunity to return. Instead, they were longing for a better country — a heavenly one. Therefore God is not ashamed to be called their God, for he has prepared a city for them.

By faith Abraham, when God tested him, offered Isaac as a sacrifice. He who had received the promises was about to sacrifice his one and only son, even though God had said to him, "It is through Isaac that your offspring will be reckoned." Abraham reasoned that God could raise the dead, and figuratively speaking, he did receive Isaac back from death. By faith Isaac blessed Jacob and Esau in regard to their future. By faith Jacob, when he was dying, blessed each of Joseph's sons, and worshiped as he leaned on the top of his staff. By faith Joseph, when his end was near, spoke about the exodus of the Israelites from Egypt and gave instructions about his bones.

By faith Moses' parents hid him for three months after he was born, because they saw he was no ordinary child, and they were not afraid of the king's edict. By faith Moses, when he had grown up, refused to be known as the son of Pharaoh's daughter. He chose to be mistreated *along with the people of God rather than to enjoy the pleasures of sin for a short time. He regarded disgrace for the sake of Christ as of greater value than the treasures of Egypt, because he was looking ahead to his reward. By faith he left Egypt, not fearing the king's anger; he persevered because he saw him who is invisible. By faith he kept the Passover and the sprinkling of blood, so that the destroyer of the firstborn would not touch the firstborn of Israel.*

By faith the people passed through the Red Sea as on dry land; but when the Egyptians tried to do so, they were drowned.

By faith the walls of Jericho fell, after the people had marched around them for seven days.

By faith the prostitute Rahab, because she welcomed the spies, was not killed with those who were disobedient.

And what more shall I say? I do not have time to tell about Gideon, Barak, Samson, Jephthah, David, Samuel and the prophets, who through faith conquered kingdoms, administered justice, and gained what was promised; who shut the mouths of lions, quenched the fury of the flames, and escaped the edge of the sword; whose weakness was turned to strength; and who became powerful in battle and routed foreign armies. Women received back their dead, raised to life again. Others were tortured and refused to be released, so that they might gain a better resurrection. Some faced jeers and flogging, while still others were chained and put in prison. They were stoned; they were sawed in two; they were put to death by the sword. They went about in sheepskins and goatskins, destitute, persecuted and mistreated— the world was not worthy of them. They wandered in deserts and mountains, and in caves and holes in the ground.

These were all commended for their faith, yet none of them received what had been promised. God had planned something better for us so that only together with us would they be made perfect. (Heb 11:1-40)

There can be no more appropriate way to close this chapter on faith than by this passage.

So, now we summarize the great truths of the gospel.

Chapter 14

The Results of the Gospel

Justification: Condemnation

Again, the gift of God is not like the result of the one man's sin: The judgment followed one sin and brought condemnation, but the gift followed many trespasses and brought justification. For if, by the trespass of the one man, death reigned through that one man, how much more will those who receive God's abundant provision of grace and of the gift of righteousness reign in life through the one man, Jesus Christ. (Rom 5:16-17)

Therefore, there is now no condemnation for those who are in Christ Jesus, because through Christ Jesus the law of the Spirit of life set me free from the law of sin and death. (Rom 8:1-2)

At that time Michael, the great prince who protects your people, will arise. There will be a time of distress such as has not happened from the beginning of nations until then. But at that time your people — everyone whose name is found written in the book — will be delivered. Multitudes who sleep in the dust of the earth will awake: some to everlasting life, others to shame and everlasting contempt. Those who are wise will shine like the brightness of the heavens, and those who lead many to righteousness, like the stars forever and ever. (Dan 12:1-3)

The gospel message can lead to either justification or condemnation. There is no middle ground.

Justification and condemnation are legal terms which define two types of judgments given in court. Justification means the person is tried, declared innocent, pardoned and set free; condemnation means that the party found guilty is sentenced in a manner and to a degree sufficient for the crime.

Our decision regarding the gospel determines the consequences of that decision.

It is clear that there will be those who will accept the gospel and those who will reject the gospel. Accordingly, the results will be uniquely different.

In one case, there will be justification; in another case, there will be condemnation. I repeat: there is no middle ground.

The results of receiving the gospel and living according to the gospel are monumental. There is good news for those who accept the gospel of Christ. Conversely, there is bad news for those who reject the gospel of Christ.

God's love is real; God's wrath is real.

His love is expressed in His justification; His wrath is expressed in His condemnation.

Those who accept the gospel will know the fullness of God's love. Those who reject the gospel will know the fullness of God's wrath.

So let us examine the consequences of our decision. First, we shall discuss those who accept the gospel of Christ and are justified. We shall conclude with those who reject the gospel and face condemnation.

- *Those who accept the gospel*

We begin with a series of beneficial results which bring new life and new hope and a new righteousness.

Consider carefully the following results of accepting the gospel of Christ.

First, we are reconciled to God:

For if, when we were God's enemies, we were reconciled to him [God] through the death of his Son, how much more, having been reconciled, shall we be saved through his life! (Rom 5:10)

Second, there is the forgiveness of sins:

This is my [Christ] blood of the covenant, which is poured out for many for the forgiveness of sins. (Matt 26:28)

Third, there is a righteousness which comes from God and is the result of our faith in God.

For in the gospel a righteousness from God is revealed, a righteousness that is by faith from first to last, just as it is written: "The righteous will live by faith." (Rom 1:17)

Fourth, there is the new birth, from above, and from God. This establishes God as our Father and we as His children. This spiritual birth is the result of receiving Christ as Savior and Lord and believing in His name.

Yet to all who received him [Christ], to those who believed in his name, he gave the right to become children of God— children born not of natural descent, nor of human decision or a husband's will, but born of God. (John 1:12-13)

Fifth, those who receive Christ will be baptized into His name and receive the gift of the Holy Spirit. Baptism symbolizes death and resurrection: we become dead to sin and alive in Christ.

Peter replied, "Repent and be baptized, every one of you, in the name of Jesus Christ for the forgiveness of your sins. And you will receive the gift of the Holy Spirit." (Acts 2:38)

Sixth, not only does our baptism lead to the gift of the Spirit and becoming a child of God, but each one of us become children of the resurrection, a resurrection which will lead to eternal life with God.

They are God's children, since they are children of the resurrection (Luke 20:36)

Seventh, those who believe in Christ will have eternal life.

Just as Moses lifted up the snake in the desert, so the Son of Man must be lifted up, that everyone who believes in him [Jesus Christ] may have eternal life. (John 3:14-15)

Eight, we become the branches attached to Christ, the true Vine. In such a state, we will bear much fruit, because of this eternal relationship.

I [Christ] am the vine; you are the branches. If a man remains in me and I in him, he will bear much fruit; apart from me you can do nothing. (John 15:5)

Ninth, the Holy Spirit will guide us into all truth. We will know the truth and it will set us free. Freedom is the result of knowing truth.

But when he, the Spirit of truth, comes, he will guide you into all truth. (John 16:13)

Tenth, we live a life in which the character is of being *in* Christ.

For in Christ Jesus neither circumcision nor uncircumcision has any value. The only thing that counts is faith expressing itself through love. (Gal 5:6)

Eleventh, we become a *new creation.*

Therefore, if anyone is in Christ, he is a new creation; the old has gone, the new has come! (2 Cor 5:17)

Twelve, those who are justified will never be condemned by God.

There is no condemnation for those who are in Christ (Rom 8:1)

Thirteen, we will never be separated from the love of God.

Nothing can separate us from the love of God in Christ Jesus our Lord (Rom 8:39)

Fourteen, the acts of the sinful nature are obvious; in the same way, the acts of the righteous nature are obvious.

Through the power of the Holy Spirit, we can have the fruit of the Spirit: love, joy, peace, patience, kindness, goodness, faithfulness, gentleness and self-control. (Gal 5:22)

Fifteen, we will receive spiritual and physical gifts so that we do that which glorifies the Trinity.

We will receive unique spiritual gifts according to our purpose (I Cor 12:8-10; Eph 4:7-13; Rom 12:3-8)

Sixteen, we will dwell with God in the New Heaven and the New Earth and the New Jerusalem.

Then I saw a new heaven and a new earth, for the first heaven and the first earth had passed away, and there was no longer any sea. I saw the Holy City, the new Jerusalem, coming down out of heaven from God, prepared as a bride beautifully dressed for her husband. And I heard a loud voice from the throne saying, "Now the dwelling of God is with men, and he will live with them. They will be his people, and God himself will be with them and be their God." (Rev 21:1-4)

Seventeen, everyone whose name is written in the book of life will be saved.

But at that time your people — everyone whose name is found written in the book — will be delivered. (Dan 12:1-2)

These seventeen truths await those who have accepted the gospel of Christ and live a life faithful and obedient to the will of God.

Not so for those who reject the gospel of Christ.

- *Those who reject the gospel*

Now, the rejection of the gospel might be direct or indirect.

A direct rejection will occur when the gospel is given and the person refuses to accept this gift of God. However, more times than not, the rejection is indirect. The person may refuse to acknowledge God, may refuse to attend church, may refuse to worship God, and just refuse to have anything to do with the Cross of Christ, may reject the Bible, may reject the sacraments (Baptism and the Eucharist), and the truths of God.

The consequences are real.

First, the person will be spiritually dead although physically alive.

Second, they will be resurrected to an eternity remote from God and one of shame and everlasting contempt.

Multitudes who sleep in the dust of the earth will awake: some to everlasting life, others to shame and everlasting contempt. (Dan 12:2)

Third, they will face the condemnation of God because of their sin.

Again, the gift of God is not like the result of the one man's sin: The judgment followed one sin and brought condemnation, but the gift followed many trespasses and brought justification. (Rom 5:16)

Fourth, They will be thrown into the lake of fire, which is the second death.

If anyone's name was not found written in the book of life, he was thrown into the lake of fire. (Rev 20:15)

So there are the differences between those who accept the gospel of Christ and those who reject the gospel.

Those who reject the gospel will be spiritually dead, which means being eternally separated from God; they will spend eternity in shame and everlasting contempt; they will face the condemnation of God; they will be thrown into the lake of fire, which is the second death.

Those who accept the gospel of Christ will be reconciled to God; their sins will be forgiven, they will be the righteousness from God; they will be born again and become the children of their Father in heaven; they will have eternal life with God; they will be branches attached to the True Vine and they will bear much fruit; they will have the Spirit to guide them into all truth; they become a new creation; they will never experience the condemnation of God; they will have the spiritual fruit of the Spirit; they can never be separated from the love of God; they will have spiritual gifts which glorify God; they will dwell with God in the new heaven and the new earth and the new Jerusalem; and, since their names are in the book of life, they will be delivered and share eternity with God.

Such are the consequences of accepting or rejecting the gospel of Christ.

Let me close with a thought regarding our decision to accept and proclaim the gospel of Christ.

When we consider the consequences of that decision, we have only to look to the life of the apostle Paul, who made such a dramatic affirmation which transformed his life.

First, the transformed life which he lived:

For through the law I died to the law so that I might live for God. I have been crucified with Christ and I no longer live, but Christ lives in me. The life I live in the body, I live by faith in the Son of God, who loved me and gave himself for me. (Gal 2:19-20)

Second, the faithfulness with which he proclaimed the gospel:

But we have this treasure in jars of clay to show that this all-surpassing power is from God and not from us. We are hard pressed on every side, but not crushed; perplexed, but not in despair; persecuted, but not abandoned; struck down, but not destroyed. (2 Cor 4:7-9)

Third, his witness to the life he had lived:

I have fought the good fight, I have finished the race, I have kept the faith. Now there is in store for me the crown of righteousness, which the Lord, the righteous Judge, will award to me on that day — and not only to me, but also to all who have longed for his appearing. (2 Tim 4:7-8)

Accepting Christ will lead to the crown of righteousness to all who have longed for His appearing.

PART 3

Epilogue

Chapter 15

Summary and Conclusions

For God so loved the world that he gave his one and only Son, that whoever believes in him shall not perish but have eternal life. For God did not send his Son into the world to condemn the world, but to save the world through him. Whoever believes in him is not condemned, but whoever does not believe stands condemned already because he has not believed in the name of God's one and only Son. This is the verdict: Light has come into the world, but men loved darkness instead of light because their deeds were evil. Everyone who does evil hates the light, and will not come into the light for fear that his deeds will be exposed. But whoever lives by the truth comes into the light, so that it may be seen plainly that what he has done has been done through God. (John 3:16-21)

I [Paul] am not ashamed of the gospel, because it is the power of God for the salvation of everyone who believes: first for the Jew, then for the Gentile. For in the gospel a righteousness from God is revealed, a righteousness that is by faith from first to last, just as it is written: "The righteous will live by faith." (Rom 1:16-17)

So now, we shall summarize God's message and His truths about the gospel of Christ.

We began by defining four major foundations of the gospel. They were: The Sovereignty of God, The Love of God, The Cross of Christ, and the Power of the Holy Spirit. Each of these four areas were discussed in some detail and provided the basis for understanding the gospel message to the fullest.

With that foundation, we have the basis to understand the *origin* of the gospel, the *content* of the gospel, the *purpose* of the gospel, the *definition* of the gospel, and the *results* of the gospel.

First, we consider the *origin* of the gospel. It is evident from Scripture that the gospel is God's plan for redemption and reconciliation of sinful man with a holy God. This plan, first announced to Abraham, had the following features: I [God] *will make you into a great nation and I will bless you; I will make your name great, and you will be a blessing. I will bless those who bless you, and whoever curses you I will curse; and all peoples on earth will be blessed through you." (Gen 12:2-3).* This gospel message to Abraham also included the *offspring* through whom all the nations will be blessed: *and through your offspring all nations on earth will be blessed, because you have obeyed me. (Gen 22:18)*

In addition, God proclaimed that it will be through the *offspring* of Abraham that this blessing would be possessed. That *offspring* was Jesus Christ. Further, the true children of Abraham are not those of physical descent, but it is those who are faithful as Abraham was faithful.

Consider Abraham: "He believed God, and it was credited to him as righteousness." Understand, then, that those who believe are children of Abraham. The Scripture foresaw that God would justify the Gentiles by faith, and announced the gospel in advance to Abraham: "All nations will be blessed through you." So those who have faith are blessed along with Abraham, the man of faith. (Gal 3:6-9)

While we saw that the origin of the gospel of Christ was through Abraham, the Scriptures also explained that the gospel was eternal.

Then I saw another angel flying in midair, and he had the eternal gospel to proclaim to those who live on the earth — to every nation, tribe, language and people. (Rev 14:6)

It is God's plan that this eternal gospel will be proclaimed throughout every age to every nation.

God told Abraham that *all the nations* would be blessed (justified) through him and his offspring. As already discussed, Jesus Christ is the offspring to whom God referred. Since the beginning of time, the Son of God was always the One through whom *all the nations* would be blessed. An adjunct to this promise is the recognized fact that *all have sinned and fall short of the glory of God (Rom 3:23).* Further, we know that Christ died on the cross for the sins of *the whole world.* And we are called to be His witnesses to the *ends of the earth* (Acts 1:8). Christ has told us that *the harvest is plentiful but the workers are few. Ask the Lord of the harvest, therefore, to send out workers into his harvest field. (Matt 9:37-38; Luke 10:2)*

God's plan was that all the nations would be blessed; His Son was the One through whom all would be blessed; all have sinned and fallen short of the glory of God; Christ died for the sins of all the world; and we are called to be witnesses to the end of the earth.

God's plan is for His entire creation; all are to be saved. In the fullness of time, it will occur.

In redemption and reconciliation, *the Lord is not slow in keeping his promise, as some understand slowness. He is patient with you, not wanting anyone to perish, but everyone to come to repentance. (2 Peter 3:9)*

God desires that all would hear the gospel of Christ, respond and be redeemed and reconciled to Him.

Second, let us consider the *content* of the gospel,

This message is centered in the Cross of Christ and His resurrection.

He is the first fruit of the resurrection; we, as the adopted children of God, are guaranteed to share in that resurrection. If He is the first fruit, then it is obvious that there will be other fruit, and we are the *other fruit.* That is the hope [certainty] of the Christian faith. That is why the Nicene Creed states: *We believe in the resurrection of the body and the life everlasting.*

The gospel, then, is the message of God, the teaching of Christianity, the redemption in and by Jesus Christ, the only begotten Son of God, offered to mankind. As the gospel is bound up in the life of Christ, His works, His signs, and the proclamation of what He has to offer are all contained in this single thought-- *good news* or *gospel*.

It is the message that Christ died for our sins, in accordance with the Scripture, that He was raised from the dead, and that He appeared to the faithful as the full and sufficient evidence of the resurrection.

Therefore, the gospel is the message of salvation that is available to all through *faith alone in Christ alone*. It is the free gift of God. For that reason, its message is one regarding our sin, our repentance, the cross of Jesus Christ, and our acceptance and appropriation of His death on the cross. The gospel is also a message of creation, in which God is redeeming His creation through the life, death, resurrection, and ascension of His Son.

The gospel, in an abbreviated form, can be summarized in the following four steps:

- A historical proclamation of the birth, death, resurrection and ascension of Jesus, as determined by Old Testament prophecies and New Testament fulfillment,
- A theological summary of the Person of Jesus Christ as both Savior and Lord,
- An invitation to acknowledge Jesus Christ as our Savior and Lord, to whom every knee shall bow and every tongue confess Him Lord, to the glory of God the Father,
- A call to acknowledge sin, to repent, and to receive the forgiveness of sins; for *by grace you have been saved through faith. (Eph 2:8)*

The message of the apostle Paul to Timothy reflected Paul's view of the gospel. Paul wrote: *and how from infancy you have known the holy Scriptures, which are able to make you wise for salvation through faith in Christ Jesus. All Scripture is God-breathed and is useful for teaching, rebuking, correcting and training in righteousness, so that the man of God may be thoroughly equipped for every good work. (2 Tim 3:15-17)*

Hear the truths that Paul presents. First, the wisdom of the Scriptures is *able to make you wise for salvation through faith in Christ Jesus*. Second, *Scripture is God-breathed—that is, God-inspired*. As the apostle Peter explained, *For prophecy never had its origin in the will of man, but men spoke from God as they were carried along by the Holy Spirit. (2 Peter 1:21)*. The Scriptures are useful for four reasons: *for teaching, rebuking, correcting and training in righteousness*. Finally, Paul identifies the purpose of Scripture: *that the man of God may be thoroughly equipped for every good work*. Remember that we are saved through faith alone (Eph 2:8-10); however, we are equipped for every good work. As the Scriptures expressed, we are saved through faith and judged by works.

There is no message in all of creation that compares with God's gospel of salvation.

It states that the God of creation sent His only begotten Son to die for the sins of the world, that He rose again from the dead, and that He ascended into heaven to sit at the right hand of God, His Father. Forgiveness of sins is offered to all who receive Him and who believe in His Name, who acknowledge and confess their sins and who repent. All who are *born again* will see and enter the Kingdom of God. God has highly exalted Jesus Christ, given Him a name above every name, and that every knee should bow and every tongue confess that He is Lord, to the glory of God the Father.

Therefore God exalted him to the highest place and gave him the name that is above every name, that at the name of Jesus every knee should bow, in heaven and on earth and under the earth, and every tongue confess that Jesus Christ is Lord, to the glory of God the Father. (Phil 2:9-11)

This is a message without parallel; it is a joyful message that we must proclaim to a *hungry* and *thirsty* world, living in darkness and having no means of salvation except through the Cross of Christ.

The gospel message is this: God first announced the gospel to Abraham, because of his obedience and faithfulness. God also made a covenant with Abraham that all the nations would be blessed (justified) through his offspring, who will be the Christ. Next, God made a promise through the prophet, Joel, that God would send forth His Holy Spirit, so that all of His people would have the divine power to accomplish every divine purpose. Further, God proclaimed through the prophet Jeremiah, that forgiveness of sins would be made available to those who repented of sins and had faith in God. Further, God decreed that His Kingdom would be an everlasting Kingdom. This was all a prelude to the Incarnation, the birth of His only begotten Son, who would come to die for the sins of the world and ratify all previous covenants and promises. The Incarnation of Christ pointed to His death on the cross, by which forgiveness of sins and redemption and reconciliation with God would result. The death of Christ led to the remarkable physical and spiritual resurrection of God where Christ is now seated at the right hand of God. As was promised, Christ will come again as King of kings and Lord of Lords. As Christ was resurrected, so shall everyone be resurrected. The resurrection will lead to the Final Judgment, at which time, everyone will receive their just reward or just punishment. The resurrection is the foundation of eternal life, for all who have received Him and believed in His name. At the completion of the Final Judgment, all things will be made new. This earth and the present heavens will pass away, and there will be a New Heaven and a New Earth and a New Jerusalem. The final portion of the good news is this: everyone whose name is written in the Book of Life will spend eternity with God in His heavenly city, the New Jerusalem. Everything will be made new.

This is the theological summary of the gospel of Christ.

Now, we turn to the purpose of the gospel,

The gospel of Christ is the ultimate expression of the love of God. Its message is salvation through faith alone in Christ alone. The eternal gospel is the good news of the coming of the New Heaven and the New Earth and the New Jerusalem, our becoming a new creation, and our spending eternity with God in His new creation.

The gospel brings joy to the heart, confidence to the spirit, renewed faith for tomorrow, and demands a response of divine love for our God and Father.

Finally, we address the *results* of the gospel.

A primary result is that we would become a new creation.

Therefore, if anyone is in Christ, he is a new creation; the old has gone, the new has come! All this is from God, who reconciled us to himself through Christ and gave us the ministry of reconciliation: that God was reconciling the world to himself in Christ, not counting men's sins against them. And he has committed to us the message of reconciliation. We are therefore Christ's ambassadors, as though God were making his appeal through us. We implore you on Christ's behalf: Be reconciled to God. God made him who had no sin to be sin for us, so that in him we might become the righteousness of God. (2 Cor 5:17-21)

The gospel of Christ is the ultimate expression of the love of God. Its message is salvation through faith alone in Christ alone. The eternal gospel is the good news of the coming of the New Heaven and the New Earth and the New Jerusalem, our becoming a new creation, and our spending eternity with God in His new creation.

Bibliography

Baker's Dictionary of Theology, Edited by E. E. Harrison (Baker Book House 1960)

Barth, Karl, *The Epistle to the Romans*, (Oxford University Press 1932

Bruce, F.F., *Commentary on Romans* (IVP 1990)

Critical Lexicon and Concordance to the English and Greek New Testament (Zondervan 1975)

Harper's Bible Dictionary, edited by M. S. Miller and J. L. Miller (Harper and Brothers 1952)

Holman's Topical Concordance (Holman Bible Publishers 1973)

International Bible Commentary, edited by F. F. Bruce (Zondervan 1986)

PC Study Bible (Biblesoft 1999)

Spurgeon, Charles Haddon, *The Power of Prayer in a Believer's Life* (Emerald Books 1993)

Stott, John R. W., *The Cross of Christ* (IVP 1986)

Basic Christianity (IVP 1978)

Understanding the Bible (Zondervan 1982)

What Christ Thinks of the Church (Lutterworth Press 1959)

The New International Dictionary of New Testament Theology, edited by Colin Brown (Zondervan 1971)

Wetmore, William H., *Him We Proclaim*, (Winepress Publishers 2006)

You Must Be Born Again (Winepress Publishers)